DATE DUE

MAY 23 1970

Organizing for Data Processing

Robert R. Reichenbach
Charles A. Tasso

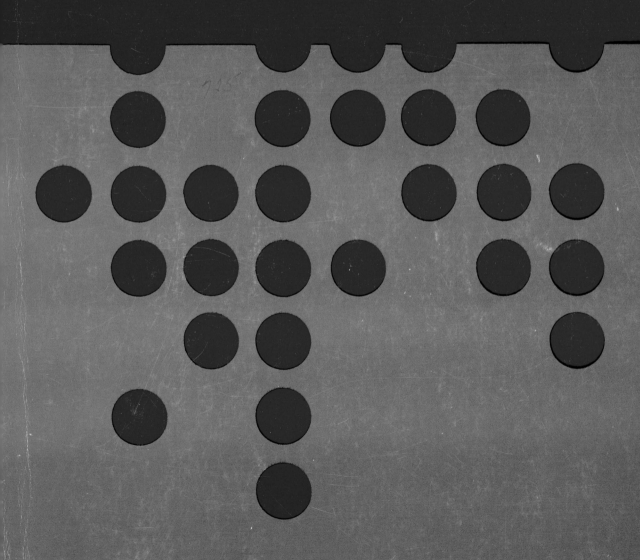

ORGANIZING FOR DATA PROCESSING

AMA RESEARCH STUDY 92

ORGANIZING FOR DATA PROCESSING

Robert R. Reichenbach
Charles A. Tasso

AMERICAN MANAGEMENT ASSOCIATION, INC.

About This Report

THE COMPANY that recognizes the contributions the computer can make to management processes, and that makes effective use of this potential, stands to reap many benefits. Information derived and processed by means of computer-based information systems can add new dimensions to management decisions, provide fresh insight into historical trends and prospective developments, and generally furnish managements with the means for delivering more supple leadership to their organizations. Used as the tool that it is, the computer can become an extension of the will of the manager and offer him a vast increase in the range of his capabilities. Certainly, as firms become larger and more complex in scope, the need for the benefits flowing from proper applications of computer technology to the process of business management will become more evident.

Managements will have to adapt their organizations to the computer, however. One cannot simply graft electronic data processing onto an existing organization and expect the results to approximate those which the computer and its uses promise. Instead, the electronic data processing (EDP) activity, as it relates to business systems, must be positioned within the organizational structure so that the activity will further the objectives of the entire organization. This is as true for the EDP function at this point in time as it was in the past for such functional specialties as industrial relations, cost control and accounting, industrial engineering, quality control, marketing, and many others. However, the extent to which the potential uses of the computer pervade all of the functions of the corporation makes this activity particularly broad in scope.

Decisions on the location of the responsibility for computer-based systems should not be left to staff specialists. These decisions are of such significance to the future operations of any company as to require the involvement of the highest levels of management. Men in these positions are able to foresee the long-term informational and decision-making needs of the corporation and to view the impact of the computer's organizational location in this light.

It is in support of this belief—that organizational decisions in the EDP area properly belong with top management—that this report is directed to members of that management group. It is designed to aid members of upper-level management in determining the organizational position of the computer responsibility within their firms, so that EDP applications to business systems will serve the aims of their companies in the most effective manner. The emphasis is on the effect of the location of the computer responsibility on the ultimate efficiency of that activity rather than on the technical aspects of computer uses for business systems or on theoretical applications of organizational science to the computer activity.

ROBERT R. REICHENBACH and CHARLES A. TASSO, under whose direction this report was prepared for the American Management Association, are senior members on the research staff of Industrial Relations Counselors, Inc. Both have been closely associated with IRC research on the organizational impact of computer technology.

Mr. Reichenbach is a graduate of the University of Nebraska (B.S.) and Cornell University (M.S.). He specializes in the organization of functions related to labor relations, public relations, and in organization and manpower planning and development. Before joining IRC, he was with Western Electric Company, served as an editor of *Business Week,* and was director of industrial relations for the Envelope Manufacturers Association. He also has lectured in labor-management relations at Fairleigh-Dickinson University and served as special consultant to the advisory committee on United States participation in the International Labour Organisation. He is a member of the Industrial Relations Research Association and the Management Development Forum.

Mr. Tasso is a specialist in behavioral science and in organization and management development. He also plans and organizes IRC's annual symposium on advanced research in industrial relations. He is the author of *Restricted Stock Options: The Intent and the Controversy,* and is a member of the American Psychological Association and the Management Development Forum.

Mr. Tasso is a graduate of St. John's University (B.B.A.) and the University of Denver (M.B.A.). He has held administrative positions with Fairchild Publications, served as a professional associate with Richardson, Bellows, Henry and Company, and was management development coordinator with American Cyanamid Company.

JOHN W. ENELL
Vice President for Research

Contents

Appendixes

Exhibits

Tables

1. Overview of the Study

WILL A COMPUTER-BASED IN-formation system function differently if the responsibility for it rests with the controller rather than with the operations vice president or a vice president of information systems? Based on the findings reported in this study, the answer is that it will. The location of the responsibility for EDP activities has a great deal to do with the nature of that responsibility and the effectiveness with which it is carried out.

Many elements of computer operations in companies today are new and are still undergoing experimentation. The concept and application of time sharing, for example, suggest a host of opportunities for more effective computer utilization. The higher speeds, greater storage capacities, and increased flexibility of third-generation computers are adding new dimensions to the application of computers to business. Less technical, but perhaps more important in terms of its implications for how the computer is used, is the question of who operates and directs the computer function. This, the subject of this study, also continues to undergo change and experimentation.

Specifically, the study has examined: (1) why responsibility in a given company is placed where it is, (2) what effect this assignment has on what the computer does and how well it does it, and (3) what the developments are that are causing changes in the location of the computer responsibility as management's need for information continues to expand, both in breadth and depth.

During the last few years top managements have given considerable attention to the question of who should direct the EDP activity. However, it was not always this way. In many companies the introduction and development of the computer and its applications were largely unplanned; as a result, the assignment of EDP responsibility was somewhat haphazard.

Highlights of the Study

In its early stages the computer was viewed as a device to facilitate performance of a specific function—accounting, research and development, engineering, production, scheduling, and others. Responsibility for the computer gravitated to the function that used it. In several companies with more than one primary use of EDP, the responsibility for computer management existed in a number of different locations. It is only recently, as top managements have come to see the computer as a powerful and flexible management tool, useful for the direction of the entire enterprise, that they have studied the impact of the location of computer responsibility. This examination has pointed up some far-reaching developments.

11

1. *Higher-level responsibility*. Responsibility for computer activities is moving toward higher levels in the corporate structure. Where such responsibility once was lodged with divisional people or with a functional unit, such as accounting, it now is found at the corporate level, and in more and more companies is independent of any specific function, with the individual heading up the computer activity reporting directly to top management—to the chairman, president, or executive vice president.

Through experience it has come to be recognized that selection of the right person to head up the computer complex is an essential ingredient in its successful functioning. However, even an excellent manager will fail to achieve optimum results unless the computer operation is properly located.

2. *Computer centralization*. As upper levels of management come to look upon the computer and the information it can provide as essentials in the process of corporate management, the responsibility for computer-based information systems becomes increasingly centralized. EDP activities of operating and functional divisions are being coordinated to a greater degree, in some companies having been pulled together into a central unit at the corporate level, thereby eliminating duplication of EDP activities among divisions and yielding a cost saving. Such EDP centralization also helps to standardize procedures. Most important, however, it permits more efficient utilization of limited numbers of EDP personnel and enables the corporate computer staff to obtain from the divisions the necessary information, in the form needed, to develop corporatewide information systems.

3. *Longer lead time*. In a substantial number of companies the technical ability to process information and to put it into the desired form has far outstripped the ability of existing methods to provide data to the computer. A widespread information system rests on a large and diverse data base and data bank. The problems associated with assimilating and digesting data, however, are relatively uncomplicated compared to those which arise when, to adapt to central computerization, divisions and other units must change their traditional methods of obtaining and using data. Unquestionably, the time needed to develop data bases accounts to a large extent for the delay American business has generally experienced in realizing the predicted benefits of computer-based information systems.

4. *Management style: effect on computer centralization*. Centralized computer activities do not necessarily lead to centralized operations and management within the company, although many divisional managers and staffs, when they learn of moves directed toward centralization, fear that their divisions will be dominated by headquarters. Because there is a danger that this will happen, contrary to the intention of higher management, EDP managers, along with the rest of management, usually try to guard against excessive quarterbacking from headquarters when up-to-the-minute, detailed information and analyses are available on divisional operations.

Instead of the computer's centralizing the company, it is the underlying, characteristic management style of the company that is the significant factor in the determination of how centralized EDP operations should be. For example, one company is using a centralized computer operation to help it decentralize its operations. A number of companies with strong historic ties to the divisional concept have left computer responsibility with the divisions and absorbed the added cost and overlap rather than seem to challenge the fundamental management philosophy. Among the study companies, centralized computer operations were found in divisionalized companies, centralized EDP operations in centralized companies, and divisional computer organizations in divisionalized companies.

5. *Computer impact on middle management*. The impact of the computer on middle managers is considerably less restrictive than has been predicted. Middle managers in companies with sophisticated information systems that use data from their functions find that they are relieved of some of the detailed routine and are able to spend the optimum time in managing.

Initially, managers of units that can benefit from EDP services may be reluctant to use the computer. Eventually, however, the problem reverses itself and becomes one of convincing these managers to obtain only the information they can and will use.

6. *Priorities for computer time*. As experience with the computer-based systems lengthens, and line managers' acceptance of EDP increases, a problem emerges that is common to EDP installations serving a variety of users. Because the time of the EDP staff and of the computers is limited, demands for computer time often outstrip availability. This means that someone has to establish priorities among potential users. The individual faced with this task is usually the manager of the EDP function, wherever it rests. He has a difficult job, and it grows more difficult as the demands for computer applications multiply.

In a large number of companies, top managements have not given the EDP manager or even the vice president the policy framework within which specific priorities can be established. Instead, the EDP manager and the user manager usually have to negotiate some satisfactory arrangement. Failing to do so, they go to a member of top management for resolution of the problem.

7. *Justification for expanded computerization*. Justification for new or additional equipment and broader computer applications once was based almost exclusively on cost savings. Of course, costs remain a critical element in decisions on computer operations, but more and more EDP staffs are finding that company managements respond readily to the ways in which a computer-based information system can enhance their ability to plan and to manage the enterprise effectively. The question becomes not "How much money will we save?" but "In addition to the money saved, how will we be able to make better decisions—and attain greater profitability?"

8. *Managerial computer know-how: effect on uses*. The fullest use of the computer as a processor of management information and as an aid to decision making has not yet been realized. Few of the men with overall responsibility for computer operations have had early, fundamental grounding in computer technology. Instead, they generally have excelled in one or another of the firm's traditional functional areas and have acquired additional knowledge about the computer. Thus they have to think in a "second language" when they think of computer uses. Younger managers at lower levels who have had computer training in high school and at the university level are now joining companies and are changing this situation. Eventually, all vice presidents of marketing, production, finance, and industrial relations, as well as of other functions, will have received training in the rudiments of EDP as part of their academic development.

9. *Communications gap*. There is also a gap in understanding between EDP personnel and general management. Managements often tend to be suspicious of the computer, regarding it as a dire threat, or they may see it merely as a limited device replacing a manual machine. Some EDP personnel, on the other hand, are unfamiliar with the basic tenets of the business in which they function and view EDP as the hub around which all else revolves. In the study companies, efforts are being made, some of which have been highly successful, to bridge this

gap from both sides. But until there is greater reconciliation of the EDP group's viewpoints with those of computer users, the potential effectiveness of the computer within the organization will not be realized.

10. *Future computer applications to management.* Overall, the promise of the computer and its application to the management process has far exceeded its accomplishments. Technologically, there are few problems aside from some relatively minor changes in software design. The lag results from the need to adapt organizations, made up of human beings, to the strict standards and procedures required for computer operations. This, enforced by the tendency of most organizations to depart only slowly from traditional ways of doing things, means that the pace of computer usage as a management tool has been keyed to human acceptance rather than to the computer's technical capability. (Interestingly, the personnel and industrial relations function is perhaps the single area in which most remains to be done in applying EDP to operations.)

But the gains that have been made by using the computer to display the entire company, or a significant part of it, at one time offer more far-reaching opportunities than have been previously available for better planning of the organization as a whole and of its structure, not only by pointing out corporate needs but also by permitting more mobile and flexible types of organization structures to function.

One of the greatest contributions already emerging from development of company-wide information systems is the invaluable training ground offered the company's potential managers in equipping them to deal with organizational problems. Many companies have already found that through serving in areas related to EDP—such as programming—and learning to use the tools of computer technology, management trainees acquire an unusual grasp of the breadth of company operations, which is invaluable in strengthening their performance as managers.

Clearly, the computer will occupy an increasingly important place in the array of tools available to managements. How effective the tool will be and how well it will be used depend to a great extent on the positioning of managerial responsibility for the computer within the organization. Since the broadest application of EDP is that which aids top-level corporate management in its tasks, it behooves management of this rank to weigh carefully the available alternatives in assigning responsibility for electronic data processing and information systems.

BASIS OF THE RESEARCH

The information reported in this study is based on multiple in-depth interviews, held between July 1966 and July 1967, with 91 executives representing 16 companies and 9 industries: airlines, chemicals and drugs, diversified heavy equipment, electrical and electronic equipment, food processing, insurance, petroleum, retailing, and utilities.

The annual sales of the smallest study company are in excess of $250 million, and several of the companies have sales of more than $1 billion; employee populations range from 7,000 to more than 100,000.

The numbers of employees engaged in activities within the computer complexes of these companies range from 5 at a corporate location in one company to more than 150 in another company. However, the total number of employees engaged in EDP activities throughout any of the companies in this survey probably exceeds 100 and, in some companies, may exceed 3,000.

Executives at three management levels were interviewed in order to gain a broad perspective on the role of the computer complex within the organization. We talked with members of top management—chief executive officers, presidents, and vice presidents—to determine what the relationship of the computer to the organization looked like from the top. We asked the people responsible for the various elements of the EDP operation to tell us about the function of the computer in relation to other functions. Finally, managers of areas that use EDP—divisional operations or functions—were asked for their views on the effectiveness of the computer. In many instances, additional clarifying information was gathered from further interviews with these executives, as well as from our continuing contacts with experts in the computer area.

The report is not based on as large a number of company experiences as could have been obtained through the use of mail questionnaires. Nor are the companies participating in the study identified. This approach was taken for two reasons. First, personal in-depth interviews are generally more effective than questionnaires for gaining insight into the actual impact on the organization, since this method of research permits points to be thoroughly explored. Second, anonymity encourages more frank and open discussion. It is our belief that the quality of information gained through anonymous interviews has advantages that far outweigh the inherent disadvantages.

The insights and facts gained from these interviews were, of course, supplemented by written material provided by the companies and analyses of published speeches, organization charts, and the like.

Finally, it should be noted that the experiences of the 16 companies cannot be considered as typical of all American industry. Nonetheless, their approaches, and the results attained, yielded a number of general conclusions that should be applicable to many companies. It is hoped that the experiences of the companies described here will be especially enlightening to those companies with, or on the verge of attaining, fairly sophisticated EDP operations and with sizable organizations within which the computer complex must fit. However, the lessons to be learned are applicable also to smaller companies that may be venturing into the area of EDP operations.

Scope of the Study

From the outset the computer has probably evoked more interest and concern, study and perplexity, confusion and disappointment than any other single tool of management. In the past ten years computers have become increasingly vital in the manufacturing process, in distribution and scheduling, in marketing, in finance, and in all of the functions of our corporations. They have altered business systems and increased the flow of information to all parts of the organization. However, in spite of the tremendous progress being made, it appears that we are only on the threshold of realizing the vast potential offered by the electronic computer or some derivative of it.

American companies now use something close to 50,000 computers in factory and office—and the end is not in sight. Daily, the public press, scholarly journals, and special publications report new developments in computer technology, and more managers become aware of the possibilities offered by the latest innovation. With so much available, it is not surprising that the managers' attention focuses on the relatively narrow area of new applications for their computer installations rather than on other areas which might offer more permanent and long-term results.

This emphasis on use, of course, is as it should be, for the computer is merely another tool available to managements in the operation of their enterprises. However, not only is this tool expensive, but the ramifications of computer applications and their impact on the total corporate organization are broader than those of most other management tools. The many possible uses of computers, ranging from their use as programmed, numerically controlled machine tools to the collection and dissemination of vast amounts of information, offer greater potential for the corporate organization as a whole than, for example, a new manufacturing device or technique. Thus the way in which this tool is introduced and assimilated into the organization has a great deal to do with the extent to which its capabilities are realized.

It was in recognition of the importance of such organizational implications that this study was undertaken. There were indications that many, if not most, companies devoted considerably more time, effort, and expense to proposed computer applications than to planning the optimum location of the computer complex, geographically and organizationally, and the means of dealing with the new relationships that would result. Consequently, it appeared that the responsibility for the computer complex was permitted to evolve in a generally unplanned fashion, which deprived management of the full benefits of computerization.

The basic hypothesis underlying this study is that the location of the computer complex within the organization will affect the complex's operations. It was postulated that the location of the complex would be a strong factor in determining computer uses in a particular company. This seemed especially likely in those instances where minimal planning had been devoted to the introduction of the computer. Also, it was assumed that the way a company's management intended to use the computer would bear heavily on its decision concerning the location of the computer complex. Moreover, it was apparent that the location of the computer complex would establish a pattern of authority and reporting relationships that would position it for the rest of the organization. This set of imposed relationships would either help the complex staff orient itself to the needs of the remainder of the organization or would restrict its ability to do so.

It was with these considerations in mind that we examined the experiences of 16 companies having a fairly long history of using computerized processes. In introducing the computer into their operations or in expanding their existing computer operations, all had dealt with the following questions—each of which must be answered in order for the computer complex to function smoothly and to serve the overall company organization effectively. The basic questions of course are: For what purpose does the company plan to use its computer? Where should responsibility for it be lodged? From the answers to these questions arise a number of other questions:

• Who should have responsibility for the computer complex?
• Where within the organizational structure should it be located?
• What form of organization would facilitate use of the computer by the various departments and divisions of the company?
• Who determines whether computer applications that are requested should, indeed, be computerized?

- How should priorities for computer service be established?
- In those companies that are considering the expansion of existing computer facilities, what special problems resulting from the computer's location and control have arisen in the past, and how have they been dealt with?

Within the study group there was considerable variation in the sophistication with which the computer was used, but all of the companies tended to be somewhat advanced in applying it to business information systems. Overall, the managements had given considerable thought to the possible use of computers for this purpose and, at one time or another, they had dealt with the question of where the computer responsibility should be located. The computer's organizational evolution from its first location to its present location and to the eventual proposed location was studied, and company rationale for selecting one location rather than another was explored. In short, company executives were asked: Where is your computer complex located? Why is it there? How did it get there? Where is it going? What are the advantages and disadvantages of the present spot?

Defining the Computer Complex

One often hears people in companies speak of "the computer" in terms of what *it* does, where *it* is located, who is responsible for *its* operation, and the like. For shorthand purposes, this designation of the whole amalgam of activities connected with the use of electronic data processing as "the computer" is fine. However, some people mean one combination of functions when they talk about the computer, while others are describing a different set of activities

when they use the term. As the phrase "computer complex" is used in this study, it means the set of specific functions that make up the total of computer activities as they relate to a management information system.

ELEMENTS OF THE COMPUTER COMPLEX

In a business organization the computer complex consists of three primary but not always discrete functions: the operation of the computer installation itself, the design and development of systems for using the capabilities of the computers, and the programming and maintenance of programs for the computer. Throughout, the term "computer complex" includes these three activities, which, the study shows, are handled in a variety of ways and combinations by companies. But not every computer complex, as an organizational entity, contains all of them.

The systems work in a company may be done within user divisions rather than in the EDP unit. Organizationally, those elements would be separate and not part of the same computer complex, but they are involved in the use of computer systems. Therefore, we include them within the concept of the computer complex. Where one or more of the elements of computer operations are located apart from most of the EDP operation, this fact is reported and its implications discusssed.

MANAGEMENT INFORMATION CONCEPT

A further refinement of the definition of the computer complex is needed. In the companies studied, computers are utilized in two broad areas, which tend to merge or overlap—the production and distribution process (which might be termed "operations" use); and the collection, processing, and dissemination of information ("information" use). These two types of application are not separate and distinct by any means. The same central processing unit may be used for both. Similarly, a single application may serve both uses, as is true when a computer which uses input from an analog device attached to fuel-oil pumps develops delivery schedules and replenishes inventory while generating output for billing purposes and for historical analysis of the impact of variable factors on fuel-oil demand.

Throughout this study, we have tried to limit our examination to the information uses of the computer and to the location of the computer complex oriented to these uses. Since the two types of application (operations and information) are not mutually exclusive, this has not always been possible. But since the location of the operations aspects of computers tends to be dictated considerably more by the particular computer application than does the location of the informational aspects, we have focused on the latter and excluded the operations aspects.

The information systems discussed here fall into two categories: limited and comprehensive. A "limited" information system is related to a specific function or purpose, although it may cover the entire corporation in fulfilling that particular function or purpose. Thus a system for accounting information or personnel information would be limited, even though it provided information on accounting or personnel throughout the entire organization.

A "comprehensive" system is composed of limited systems and includes cross-functional and interlevel information about the company as a whole. Through such a system the potential impact of a particular event, such as an increase in the price of the primary raw product, on each aspect of the company's operations can be simulated if the system provides a simulation model. Or such a system can provide comprehensive information in summarized form about the

company's operation as a whole, in order to enable management to decide among alternatives. A comprehensive system is based on the data used in the limited systems. These data, in assembled form, are referred to as the "data base," both for the limited systems and for the comprehensive system, depending on the extent of the data's coverage.

One further qualification is necessary. Because of the constantly expanding and shifting nature of computer applications, some of the material reported in this document reflects steps now being taken by the study companies—or that were being taken by them at the time of the study—toward the creation or expansion of an information system for management. No company in the study has a "total management information system," as the term is used frequently today. In fact, while companies may develop comprehensive management information systems yielding a vast amount of information about the operations of the enterprise, the accomplishment of a *total* information system is not possible, almost by definition. Even if all of the pertinent information necessary to create a *total* system were obtained and processed, the very existence of the *total* system, and the information derived from it, would become the basis for constructing another *total* system by using this information; the latter's output, in turn, would become the basis for another *total* system, and so on.

In terms of the systems it has today, each of the companies is a long way from having the type of systems it envisions for the future. A few companies, and more divisions within companies, have factored information on a significant number of activities into their systems. Yet even these systems do not have the coverage that the companies are striving for. However, the experience of the study companies in planning and developing systems, even though the systems are not fully developed, is as valuable for study as it would be if the systems were completely operational.

RELATIONSHIP OF EDP AND MANAGEMENT INFORMATION SYSTEMS

It should be noted also that we found the terms "data processing," or "EDP," and "information systems" are used almost synonymously. The reason is that every company, except one, that has a developing management information system has assigned the responsibilities for data processing and for construction and operation of the information system to the same spot. This is true no matter where the responsibility for the two exists. It is as true in one study company, where the vice president of information systems has overall responsibility for information sources, information systems, computer operations, operations research and systems planning, as it is in another, where the responsibility exists at the assistant controller level.

In several of the study companies the development of a broad, computer-based management information system is, at present, secondary to the use of the computer largely for accounting operations. But in such cases, where the computer responsibility lies with a controller, usually under the direct supervision of an assistant controller, the responsibility for developing the information system also rests with the controller. In short, the same combination of functions—EDP and information systems—is found whether the computer complex is located at the vice presidential level or at the assistant controller level, in divisions or at a central location.

In a practical sense, then, it is not worthwhile to discuss the location of these two highly interrelated activities—data processing and information systems work—and their impact on the organization as though

they should be distinguished and treated separately.

Assessing the Effectiveness Of the Computer Complex

When we examined the experience of the study companies, several broad questions bearing on location and control were explored to determine their impact on the effectiveness with which the systems we studied operate:

- How do computers relate to existing information systems when they are introduced?
- How does the computer's organizational location help or hinder efforts to generate relevant data?
- How is the computer's location viewed by management and employees?
- How have management's attitudes affected the computer complex?

HOW DOES THE COMPUTER AFFECT EXISTING INFORMATION SYSTEMS?

It is important to recognize that an information system, which tends to cut across functional lines and to combine previously separate data, is not necessarily the product of electronic data processing. Information systems existed long before EDP came on the scene; EDP has simply permitted the creation of more extensive and elaborate systems, which, in turn, required an "engineered" or systems approach. Thus with EDP, many companies that already had information systems could extend their systems considerably in speed and coverage. If they did, however, there would inevitably be an impact on organizational relationships. Here lies the dilemma. Can responsibility for the establishment and maintenance of the mushrooming information system, which cuts across the organization, continue to reside in the spot established for it when it was geared to the desk calculator and the typewriter? Will the mere presence of the computer complex in a particular location within the organization act to restrict future computer applications and render the computer a less flexible tool than it could be if it were located elsewhere?[1]

A number of avenues are open for the admission of EDP into information systems:

1. Computers can simply utilize and formalize existing information channels and techniques. This approach would require the least realignment of functional and organizational relationships and, hence, would appear to many companies to be desirable. If this is done, then the location of the computer probably will cause few repercussions outside of the area to which it is assigned, and the benefits to management will be limited largely to improvements in existing methods.

2. Through the computer, existing information channels and techniques can be expanded considerably, both in terms of the quality of information derived and the areas covered. On the surface this approach might appear to offer many of the advantages of EDP while causing minimal organizational disruption. However, as a number of companies are learning, this avenue can also create internal conflict while withholding the benefits of a full-scale, computer-based information system.

3. The third course is for management to develop and initiate new channels of information to form the system. Knowledge of what is needed by management, and what can be provided by an information system, coupled with an understanding of the capabilities of EDP equipment, must go into the determination of these new channels and how they will be used. As at least one writer has pointed out, the design of a computer-based system that will closely fit management's needs is a continuing task that causes many companies difficulty.[2]

DOES LOCATION AFFECT THE RELEVANCY OF DATA?

At the outset of the study it was hypothesized that the organizational location of the data processing and/or information system function would play a significant role in determining the system's relevance to management needs. It appeared that assignment of computer responsibility to an existing function that had responsibility for all or part of the existing information system might result in the use of computerized data to support and strengthen that function. On the other hand, where the responsibility created a new and separate function, it seemed possible that the information generated might consist more of spectacular demonstrations of computer prowess than of processing of data needed by management. Neither of these cases would yield truly relevant management information. Obviously, neither of these approaches necessarily carries with it the flaws listed here. But as extremes that might occur, they require exploration in this study. Certainly, the system must work so that management will not be forced "to hunt through a haystack of irrelevant information in its reports in order to find for itself the needle of pertinent fact."[3]

---

[1] Frank Jasinski, in addressing himself to this issue, states that "a change in production or technology affects organizational relationships." See "Adapting Organization to New Technology," *Harvard Business Review,* January-February 1959, pp. 79–86. The same can be said of a change or introduction of the EDP process in the information system, except that the impact will be even greater.

[2] James D. Gallagher, *Management Information Systems and the Computer,* Research Study No. 51, American Management Association, New York, 1961, pp. 11–13.

[3] Gerald L. Phillipe, "What Management Really Wants from Data Processing," *Data Processing To-*

WHAT IS THE IMPACT OF INDIVIDUAL ATTITUDES ON LOCATION?

The formal, charted, organizational relationship of the computer complex to the existing organization is only one aspect of the location question. Another consideration which must be taken into account is the impact on, and reactions of, the individual to which the responsibility is assigned. A given management may decide that, from the standpoint of the company's operations and proposed computer applications, the computer complex should be assigned to the controller's function. But what if the controller in that company regards the computer simply as an enlarged accounting or calculating machine and can see no application for it beyond the accounting department?

In this study we were interested in discovering this sort of situation and in learning how companies dealt with the problem of individual attitudes and the ways in which these attitudes enhanced or impeded the results expected from locating the computer in a particular department.

WHAT MANAGEMENT ATTITUDES ARE MOST SIGNIFICANT?

Knowledge of the attitudes of top management toward the computer and its potential was also considered essential to an analysis of the effectiveness of the computer within the organizational structure of a particular company. Recognizing that assignment of the EDP process to a specific place within the organization might reflect a certain top management attitude, we endeavored to ascertain the attitudes, the interest, and the commitment of the managements of the participating companies to increased

day: A Progress Report, Management Report No. 46, American Management Association, New York, 1960, p. 12; cited in Gallagher, *ibid.*, p. 59.

computer utilization for information purposes. Despite the informational capabilities of computers, it appeared evident that they would function as the management of that company permitted, and that they would be placed within the organization to function in the prescribed fashion. It also seemed likely that top management's involvement in the whole EDP question would bear heavily on the objectives sought by the company through utilization of the computer.

DOES PAST EXPERIENCE WITH THE COMPUTER AFFECT LOCATION?

Other factors, such as the company's traditional style of organization, its product mix, and its geographical coverage were also examined for their effect on the company's approach to the location and organization of the EDP operation. Most important, however, was the length of time the company had had computers and how it used them. An oversimplified way of referring to this is the company's *degree of sophistication* with respect to computers.

The development of increased computer flexibility and capacity continues at a dazzling pace, sometimes even catching up with some of the more imaginative claims of vendors. The corollary development of computer utilization in companies tends to be somewhat uneven, with one company using the experiences of others to push forward a bit, then becoming the source of experience for another company's leap forward. Today, however, technical developments within the computers themselves are taking place so rapidly, and technical competence within many companies has reached so high a level, that many companies are generating their own leaps forward. Thus considerable time was spent with participating executives, tracing the history of the computer and its applications within the company and exploring expected future developments to determine how far down the road the company was in comparison with other companies, in terms of where the company itself wanted to go.

The data processing manager in a highly divisionalized company took note of this time phenomenon when he stated that he had to "hard-sell" new applications to divisions which have had computers for a short period of time, while he found that those with longer experience required no such selling.

Summary of Study Conclusions

The results of the study are presented in the following section. These conclusions have been grouped under four major headings:

- Organizational location and the effectiveness of the computer complex.
- The evolution of the computer and its uses.
- The use of the computer for organizational planning.
- Relationships with management.

For purposes of amplification or explanation, each conclusion is followed by a brief discussion of the supporting reasons. Considerably more detail on the conclusions appears in the body of the report.

A key philosophical point which has been fully underscored by our findings underlies the entire body of conclusions. This is that the computer is merely a management tool (although a powerful and flexible one) which does not necessarily alter the style or philosophy of a particular management but, rather, contributes to the ability of management to make desired changes in method to bring the management system into conformity with prevailing management philosophy.

This view enables management to make the most effective use of information, which is obtained in greater quantity, in less time, and in more usable form through the computer than through any other means. If any one thread ran consistently through the discussions with the people interviewed in the study, it was that the computer does nothing more, or less, than the persons who control it want it to. Though this may seem so obvious as to be a cliché, it is a fundamental point in any consideration of the computer in a business organization—and a point too frequently ignored.

ORGANIZATIONAL LOCATION AND THE EFFECTIVENESS OF THE COMPUTER COMPLEX

The basic conclusion of our study is that *there is a very real relationship between the location of the computer complex within the organization and its effectiveness in meeting company needs.* In case after case in the study companies the location of the data processing/information system function has been moved within the organization because its job, in management's judgment, could be more effectively accomplished in one location than in another. Similarly, those companies which had given considerable thought to future uses of the computer generally located the complex so that it would be able to achieve those uses. Some corollary conclusions can be drawn from this overall conclusion.

Responsibility for the computer complex, including information systems, should be apart from any existing traditional function. The function should report directly to top management. Although sound arguments are presented for opposing views on this question, there is a gradual trend toward a high-level, separate data processing/information system function. Except for those companies with special characteristics that make it impractical to establish the computer complex as a separate function reporting to management, this is a sound tendency. While control is clearly one of the objectives of an information system, over-emphasis on control tends to retard planning for future applications.

Location of the computer complex in a functional area has two results:

1. It creates the possibility, if not the probability, that the computer will be used largely by that function at the expense of other functions and, ultimately, at the expense of the company.
2. It places the computer in a subsidiary position within the existing function, making it difficult for other functions to have access to the computer. Even a particularly energetic controller may be hampered in his efforts to develop a general-purpose, computer-based information system by the relatively limited view of the controller's function held by some nonfinancial executives.

Aside from these two results, the standardization and configuration required for a computer-based information system can be achieved more economically and effectively through a high-level function devoted entirely to assembling, processing, and disseminating information. There are some exceptions to this general conclusion. In a company where management's need for, and support of, data processing activities is weak, a separate function reporting to that management would not be successful; however, a data processing unit located within an existing function might operate very effectively, as the experience of one study company in such a situation showed. But if and when the views of top management change, as they have in several of the companies in this study, the installation of a separate data processing function is much more likely to prove successful.

Much of the blame for the internal controversy over whether the computer should be part of a traditional function or exist independently has been attributed to the quest for power inherent in managing the "black box," but there is more to the problem than personal power struggles. The pros and cons are summed up best by executives from different companies. One, a controller, argues:

> It's a question of accountability. No one has ever been able to figure out how to take the business-integrating function out of the finance area. Control *is* financial data. But it's more than that, too; it's physical items, quantities, and numbers as well as dollars. All of this is control data. The information system is synonymous with the control system. Under a separate setup, where everybody uses a central computer facility to develop his own systems, the financial head has no control over the system's input; he's just a scorekeeper. But under such an arrangement, the top guy in that operation wouldn't be able to do *one* thing more, or in a broader way, than the finance guy would be able to do if he retained control. Sure, you can reorganize and take the data processing out of the controller's office and call it "wheeling and dealing" or anything you want. But you will still have the same control problems you had before. In the final analysis, as long as finance has responsibility for the business-integrating function in the company, as it does, finance has to be responsible for the integrity of the data.

A divisional data processing manager expressed this view:

> Under no circumstances should the management information system be under the controller. Controllers constantly squeeze the buck at the expense of the system. They're always taking potshots from the outside at something they don't really understand. The situation at headquarters here (where the information system is under the controller) is highly unfortunate.

From another data manager, at the corporate level, in a separate function reporting directly to the company president, comes this observation:

> Given people with the same degree of competence, there is no question of the wisdom of making the data processing and information systems function a separate corporate staff function. The ease and effectiveness with which these activities go on separately, compared to what it would be like under the accounting area, is like comparing night and day. It makes so much sense to have these as a separate function. A general-purpose information system must be cross-functional and interlevel. A separate organization can accomplish this in a way that accounting cannot. The type of team we are putting together here can be infinitely more effective where it is than it could be in accounting or in any other functional area.

Neither the presence of the computer itself, the location of the computer complex, the centralization of computer activities, nor a combination of these three need have any impact on the traditional form of the corporate structure. One of the primary sources of resistance to the computer on the part of divisional managers, especially operating managers, is the fear that the computer will centralize all authority, control, decision making, and other aspects of management in the headquarters office. To a degree, there is some basis for this fear. Eventually, the availability of detailed operational data on a real-time or nearly real-time basis, and the use of telecommunications, cathode-ray tubes for display, and executive chartrooms might induce top management to become more involved in operations and decision making at lower levels than is possible in most companies today. Realizing this, some managers see in these developments an inevitable move toward centralized information gathering, control, and decision making.

Such fears are fed to a considerable extent by *the EDP approach to the organization.* This approach, evident in much of the writing on the subject and advanced by some EDP people, views the data processing operation as tending to shape the organizational structure, usually in the direction of centralization. Data processors have been heard to say that other functions in the company "ought to be made to supply the information we want the way we need it." But is there a real basis for the assumption that the computer leads to centralized management? We think not.

As to the computer's effect on information gathering, there can be no doubt that there is a trend toward centralization of information-gathering activities. Centralized information does not, however, necessarily mean centralized management. There will be greater centralization of control and decision making only if management wants this centralization. On the other hand, if management wants decentralized management and operations, it can use a computer-based information system, even a highly centralized one, to help attain this goal. Nearly all of the centralized data processing operations covered here exist in decentralized and divisionalized companies. Moreover, one company chairman is currently using a centralized data processing/information system function to move his company from a strongly centralized position to a decentralized one. Thus the decentralization or centralization of the computer function may run counter to the company's method of operating, but the decentralization or centralization of control will reflect the philosophy of company management rather than any pressures from the computer function.

There is evidence that most managements may be unwilling to exercise as much control and detailed decision-making capability as the computer will some day make available. Top management must focus on business building. Moreover, at present, future management people receive their training in the operating divisions and subsidiary companies; here they learn, make decisions, and make some mistakes. If the freedom to make all but the smallest decisions were moved to the higher-management levels, this training area would be eliminated. Middle and junior management must be free to make decisions or else there will be no basis on which to gauge their results and abilities. The members of management we interviewed are keenly aware of this need. It must be kept in mind also that computers cannot make decisions but can provide sound information on which people can make them.

A centralized computer facility and information system permits more efficient utilization of limited numbers of EDP personnel in meeting the needs of user organizations. The trend toward centralized, corporate-level data processing and information systems raises the question of how EDP personnel will be made sufficiently knowledgeable about divisional problems and operations to develop the best systems for the divisions. Some of the study companies have taught EDP personnel about the divisions, and others have taught divisional people about data processing. While both approaches have been used successfully, the latter system seems to work more effectively. Moreover, to overcome the general shortage of EDP personnel, companies are discovering that non-EDP employees can be trained as programmers and, within a year or two, as systems engineers or analysts. This should permit considerable systems development work to be done within the user organization itself. The newly trained EDP people not only will require relatively little assistance from data processing core employees, but in the long run, this approach should lead to better rapport between the EDP unit and the users of its services, as well as

to results that are better tailored to the users' needs.

EVOLUTION OF THE COMPUTER AND ITS USES

In general, companies with comparable levels of sophistication and length of computer experience have arrived at much the same judgments regarding the evolution of the computer complex in the organization.

Very soon after feasibility studies have been made and the computer has been introduced into the company, one individual, rather than a committee, must be appointed by management to make decisions on computer acquisition, on the specific uses for the computer, and to coordinate EDP activity. This general conclusion is valid regardless of the extent to which immediate uses for the computer are envisioned. The assignment of individual responsibility, rather than committee responsibility, is necessary whether the computer is viewed as a tool to be used on a corporatewide basis or as one to be used primarily or solely to meet the needs of one or more divisions. In either case the location of responsibility with one individual is a prime requisite for getting the action needed to carry out the mission set for the computer operation.

A number of executives interviewed during the study reported that the committee approach to the introduction of the computer did not work, because it became an avenue for avoiding decisions, and that a strong man was needed to achieve results.

In many of the companies in this study, the first evaluation of what the computer could do for the company came from a feasibility study made by a committee. Often, after completion of the feasibility study, the committee continued in existence as a steering committee to assist in the introduction of the computer. In nearly every instance, in the absence of any individual authority to make final determinations, the work of the committee bogged down, and almost without exception it was replaced or supplemented by an individual who had been given the specific assignment of launching the computer project. In some companies the executive so involved became known as "Mr. Computer," the computer "czar," or the data processing "dictator." The fact that these terms are applied by members of top management suggests the strong desire within the company for prompt action.

On the other hand, the experience of the "computer pioneer" in several companies shows what can happen to an employee who becomes identified with the computer too soon. In general, the men who pioneered in the use of computers in these companies have been bypassed and assigned to advisory roles. There are several reasons for this.

First, like most pioneers, they stepped on toes and generated resistance to themselves as well as to their projects. Frequently, being more attuned to the electronics of computers than to the dynamics of human relationships, they became obstacles to the further progress of their own ideas.

Second, most of these men were hardware-oriented. They knew the intricacies of the equipment but had only limited knowledge of applications. Often they were unable or unwilling to move on to the broader applications that became necessary as the computer gained acceptance.

Third, out of their conviction of the importance of the computer, some pioneers gained a top-level reporting relationship before management really understood or accepted the computer. Consequently, no real support existed, and efforts to expand the uses of the computer were ineffective because of objections or obstacles thrown up by the divisions and other managers. Thus the importance of the identification of the key computer executive by management, rather than his attempting to claim this role for himself—a matter of timing—is an important ingredient for the success of early computer activities.

Selection of the proper manager and the optimum location for the computer are mutually supportive. A manager who is not equipped to handle the data processing operation will not succeed even when the complex is in the right organizational location. Conversely, a strong EDP manager will be unable to get the best results from the computer if its location makes his position ineffective. Often, early selection of the right man to head the computer complex can lead to a solution of the location problem. For example, in two different companies the computer responsibility was given to very capable men when computers were first introduced. In both cases these individuals proved to be strong spokesmen for the merits of computerization, and their ability contributed greatly to the advanced computer-based management information systems found in these companies today and to the resultant location of the computer complex where it could best meet the company's needs. Each man is now president of his company, and his assignment to this position stemmed, to a large extent, from his computer experience.

The nature of a company's business significantly affects the ease and timing of its progress in the use of computers for information purposes. The study companies that were among the first to use computers and to anticipate the value of an information system tend to have several broad characteristics in common. Among them are:

1. *A strong scientific, engineering, or research and development orientation.* Companies that manufacture such sophisticated products as chemicals and electric and electronic equipment generally have the type of employee who is already equipped to grasp the complexities of the computer and to see its possibilities. Much the same is

true of companies that emphasize research and development. Often in these companies the computer was introduced in engineering or in research and development, largely because employees here were quick to grasp the concept of the computer and to see how it might apply to their operation.

2. *A high-volume operation, with high turnover and short lead time on orders,* such as a retailing company or a food processing and marketing organization, which sees a way to reduce the cost of handling the vast amount of detail and paperwork that goes with its business, usually jumps at this opportunity. If the product's unit price is low and the profit margin is narrow, the incentive is even greater. Among the study companies, those in this category were among the early users of the computer. Most of them no longer view the computer solely as an aid in cutting costs, but as an aid in speeding paperwork, in maintaining the same short lead time while processing orders faster, and in reducing the customer order lead time.

Two of the study companies, which are among the most advanced in computer applications for information purposes, are in this group. While they did not turn to the computer quite as early as those companies with scientific and engineering employees, their search for new and better informational computer applications appears to have been more persistent and imaginative. In the low unit-profit companies the informational yield of a computer-based system in giving the company a cost advantage is more easily seen than in companies with a higher unit-profit volume and is more crucial to the company's business. In high unit-profit companies, including those manufacturing heavy equipment, technical equipment, electronic devices, or other products, the computer is seen as a production aid that controls tools, helps to schedule production, assists in quality control, and the like. Informational applications of the computer may be regarded as supplementary to production operations.

3. *A large number of customers.* Many of the same factors noted above apply in such companies as retailing, insurance, and food marketing, in which the sheer physical problem of processing a large volume of orders and accounts can be assisted through computer applications. This type of operation usually needs effective forecasting, which computers can provide through linear programming, projections of past data, and other techniques. Much imaginative work has been done by the larger companies of this type in developing the forecasting possibilities of the computer.

Use of the computer should not be justified solely or primarily on the basis of cost savings. In the beginning, nearly all of the study companies justified acquisition of a computer almost exclusively on the basis of the future savings in costs. While this might have been an adequate basis for introducing first-generation computers into the organization, it is only one factor today, in view of the great expense and vast capabilities of the third-generation computers. Using cost saving alone as the criterion for acquiring a computer or expanding its use can result in a decision against the computer, which, if it were introduced, might point the way to changes that would put immediate cost considerations into a secondary position.

All of the more advanced companies, including those in the study group, now go beyond immediate cost-saving considerations in justifying further computer applications and acquisition of additional hardware. Several companies have recently altered their computer facilities to accommodate third-generation computers and are now spending more on electronic data processing than previously, with, in the immediate term, no actual increase in the return on data processing activity. The moves were made because of the potential for systems that would give greater service to company management. The emphasis, instead of on cutting costs, was on what the computer could do to increase profits, improve management flexibility, and provide better bases for important management decisions. The cost factor was considered in the light of the potential benefits of a computer or its application weighted against the cost of providing it.

Some of the savings realized peripherally by the computer's presence are difficult to measure. In company after company the mere existence of the computer had fostered a systems approach to problems and procedures, even where the computer might not be directly involved. People who had become accustomed to looking at their problems and assigned tasks in the logical, systematic way required by the application of computer techniques also tended to view all of their operations in the same systematic way. That this attitude has improved practices and procedures is accepted. What the savings have been is not calculable.

USE OF THE COMPUTER FOR ORGANIZATION PLANNING AND MANAGEMENT DEVELOPMENT

The vast majority of computer applications in operation in companies today deal with discrete factors—dollars, units of production, orders, inventory items, and the like. Applications to more abstract or conceptual purposes are relatively scarce, although more and more companies are moving toward these uses. One of the major areas in which computer applications can

be of immense benefit to companies is the management of the human resources and the structuring of the work of the enterprise. But neither the personnel function in many companies nor the organization-planning function is among the heaviest users of the computer. The results achieved by the companies that have used computers for structuring the human side of the business, and the plans of others to do so, merit some conclusions about the application of computer technology to this sector of the firm.

Computer-based information systems of a corporatewide nature enhance the effectiveness of organization planning by bringing about greater opportunities to relate the organization structure, as an entity, to the overall needs and objectives of the business. Here, we are not speaking of direct applications of computer technology to the organization-planning process, but of how the products of computer-based information systems can be used by organization planners. As Gordon Donhowe, director of planning, the Pillsbury Company, has observed, there is little to report on how computer technology is being applied to the organization-planning process, but the actual use of computer technology in industrial organizations "has very real and immediate implications for organizational planning."[4]

Organization planning has suffered, to a high degree, from the absence of an integrated, theoretical approach to it and from the continuing difficulty, in practice, of relating the organization plan to often imprecise and shifting corporate objectives and needs. The current generation of computers offers little prospect of filling the theoretical gap. But comprehensive information systems, utilizing computer technology, do

---

[4] Gordon M. Donhowe, "Organization Planning and the Impact of Technology," *Computer Technology—Applications for Management,* Industrial Relations Counselors, Inc., New York, 1967, pp. 81–82.

hold forth the promise of a clearer vision of the company and organization as a whole, or as most of a whole. As these information systems provide an increasing number of parts to the total picture of the enterprise, and as greater use is made of models and various forms of simulation, organization planning will be able to take into account, and adapt itself to, an increasingly larger part of the whole.

To the extent that information systems permit the diagraming of clearer corporate needs and objectives, the organization-planning unit will be in a position to plan and implement needed changes in the organizational structure. Thus it is not the computer itself or its technology that aids the organization-planning process, but the information derived through systems oriented to the computer. The view of the corporation as a whole, however, is especially beneficial to the organization-planning activity.

Another interaction of the computer and the organization should be mentioned. Somewhat paradoxically, the information derived from computer-based systems and used in companies today fosters a new flexibility or instability in organizational structure while, at the same time, engendering a degree of stability within the corporate framework that supports organizational flexibility.

Rapid changes in technology, more than a few stemming from computer applications, require that both management and the structure of the organization be responsive to change and be able to adapt quickly. For this reason many of the established tenets of institutional design, which tend to immobilize rather than stimulate, are being abandoned. In some companies, especially those in defense and space-related industries, new forms of organization already have emerged. Small, multidiscipline task forces, formed to solve a specific problem, are being created and are organizing themselves, accomplishing their tasks, and dissolving. Thus, mobile organizational structures[5]—or nonstructures—are replacing the traditional authorities and reporting relationships and erasing the historical sense of organizational rigidity.

Advances in the informational uses of computer technology have been instrumental in achieving the conditions under which such mobile structures can function; to this extent, they have contributed to the flexibility or instability of the new organizational forms. At the same time, information systems, once established and maintained, provide the stability necessary to the continuation of the enterprise in its administrative and informational aspects. Both this stability and the flexibility of new organization structures would seem to be essential in some companies today—and in more companies in the future.

Service in an area closely related to electronic data processing, such as systems development, or in the electronic data processing function itself, is excellent training for future managers. In addition to the education in computer concepts provided for managers and potential managers (we will go into more detail on this later), some of the study companies consider computer experience, because much of it is cross-functional, extremely useful in developing future managers. Such experience, especially if it is connected with systems development, offers an unusual opportunity for managers to acquire a grasp of a broad range of the company's operations. In addition, this experience permits future managers to become

---

[5] These are referred to by such descriptions as *organic, organic-active, free-form,* and others. See, for example, Donhowe, *op. cit.,* p. 89; Warren Bennis, *Changing Organizations,* McGraw-Hill Book Company, Inc., New York, 1966, p. 118; and Max Ways, "Tomorrow's Management: A More Adventurous Life in a Free-Form Corporation," *Fortune,* July 1966, pp. 84–87, 148–150.

familiar with computers, a tool that they will use increasingly as managers. More and more companies have come to see the value of this type of training.

Moreover, EDP experience for rising managers has a beneficial side effect. The interchange of personnel between the data processing operation and the user areas, especially at the managerial level, results in greater understanding of one another's needs and problems, leading to greater rapport between the units and paving the way for more effective applications of the computer to the users' needs.

Computer-based information systems and modern communications techniques can strengthen middle management's power to make decisions. A vast amount has been written on the subject of the impact of the computer on middle management, the inevitability of central control with the advent of real-time information systems, and the like. Indeed, greater computerization of information does carry the seeds of centralization, perhaps eventually complete centralization. Whether these seeds sprout and mature, however, depends not upon the information system, but upon the managements employing it. As is stressed throughout this document, it is unlikely that centralization will grow to anything like the extent that has been prophesied.

One reason for some current efforts to centralize is management's disenchantment with decentralization, which grows out of the difficulty of maintaining the orientation of the divisional activities toward those of the corporation as a whole. Computer-based information systems, using telecommunications, effectively remove much of this problem, at least from the purely mechanical side. Thus if management favors remaining decentralized, it has the means to do so.

Another reason for our belief that strong centralization will not occur is that, as discussed earlier, it would remove from the rising executive the opportunity for valuable managing experience. Computer-oriented information systems can be utilized to make these managing experiences even more meaningful for middle managers. Many executives—at both top and middle levels—reported that computer applications had relieved the middle manager of much of the administrative routine of his job and freed him to do what he supposedly was paid to do—manage. A number of chief executives indicated considerable satisfaction with the upgrading of the decisions being made by middle managers, both in quality and in the nature of the decisions undertaken. Many middle managers (middle in the corporation but top in a division) have thoroughly grasped the decision-making assistance, such as simulation and Bayesian decision theory, to be derived and are using it effectively to broaden the area in which they make decisions and to improve the quality of those decisions. In short, computer technology does not appear to threaten middle management with annihilation; instead, its uses are strengthening this stratum of management.

RELATIONSHIPS WITH MANAGEMENT

Although there are operational aspects to information systems that are essential to the conduct of the business, such as billing, purchasing, and inventory, which can be accomplished in the process of data collection, the big payoff in these systems comes through their application to the process of directing the enterprise. As one student of the decision-making process has put it:

> Making decisions is hard work. Managers who are faced with too many difficult decisions too fast often suffer physically and mentally. . . . It seems no wonder, in this age of rapid communication and transportation, that managers and scientists are striving to find mathematically rational systems to take over at least some of the load of

stressful decision making in a divided world.[6]

If information systems are being developed for management's ultimate use in making decisions, it is important that some sort of *rapprochement* be reached by management and the information systems people. Some conclusions on this and on the needs which must be met before this accommodation will take place are discussed below.

Participation by management in the planning of informational applications will speed acceptance of the computer, improve its utilization, and help configure applications to management needs. The import of this conclusion is obvious to any functional manager who has tried to broaden the coverage of his activity. Its importance has not always been appreciated by data processing personnel, however. Because of the resistance sometimes displayed by management, data processing managers frequently attempt to shield members of management from the computer people, who speak a different jargon and who tend to have a different view of the EDP operation and the company than that of management. This may be a workable approach as the use of the computer gains momentum, but the eventual answer will lie not in shielding management but in educating it in the concepts of the computer and its uses.

Nearly every company in the study exposes its executives to some form of educational experience with computers. Most data processing managers agreed, however, that there remains an immense amount of educating to be done in this area. To the extent, then, that top management and other members of management can be edu-

cated beyond the superficial stage to become more aware of the possibilities of computer technology, the data processing and information systems operations can be better directed toward the overall goals of the company and its management.

Information involving the computer should be designed at the outset for use by the highest levels of management. Clearly, there are many exceptions to this conclusion. Some systems or parts of systems will never be applicable to top management needs, but, in general terms, broad-gauged information systems should be geared as soon as possible to the needs of upper-level management. Some of the data processing/information systems managers in the study companies were convinced that this would be a dangerous approach—that it would be a long time before the upper echelons of the company were ready to derive any benefit from computer-based information systems. One corporate data processing head stated that he was stressing computer applications for levels below top management, because, he said, top management knew little about computers and was not prepared to use computer applications. Yet the chairman of that company showed detailed knowledge of what was happening with computers and information systems in his organization and displayed an interest in future developments that would have amazed his data processing manager.

Several other situations were encountered where the data processing activity, geared largely to limited or operating applications, had to be changed drastically when management began to request results of systems applications. The data being obtained were not in a form that would be useful or meaningful to top management, so the focus had to be shifted from a narrow to a broader approach to meet management's needs. Had the original systems been designed with this possible application in mind, much of

[6] Merrill M. Flood, "Sequential Decisioning," in Robert E. Machol, ed., *Information and Decision Processes,* McGraw-Hill Book Company, Inc., New York, 1960, p. 34.

the backing and filling could have been avoided.

Future managers, solidly grounded in computer uses through their early schooling, will begin to utilize computers so that their potential will be approached. Nearly all of the data processing managers or executives responsible for the overall data processing/information systems activity in the study companies are men in their late 30's to mid-40's who have solid experience in their companies and who have added an acquired knowledge of computer technology and information systems to that experience. Many of these men are doing outstanding work with computer-based information systems, but they are working in an essentially unfamiliar medium. Their thought processes and ways of approaching problems were formed in precomputer days; moreover, they are serving user units headed by managers whose views on the computer range from curiosity, through indifference or skepticism, to outright antagonism. These conditions have tended to limit the use of the computer for informational purposes to a level well below its potential.

In the near future, executives in marketing, engineering, accounting, and other functions will be familiar with the intricacies and promises of the computer by dint of the training they will have received in school. More and more colleges and universities, along with high schools and other secondary schools, include instruction in computer use, coupled with actual "hands on" experience. Even a few elementary schools have integrated computers with teaching methods, so that a fifth-grade class, for example, can make intricate celestial computations by using a predetermined formula and a data processing terminal. As these youngsters become managers they may regard the computer as an aid to the thought process in much the same way that pencil and paper is regarded today. Such

an attitude, permeating the organization, should create an atmosphere in which the full potential of computer technology for business operations may be realized, or at least closely approached.

Management must establish broad guidelines for using the computer within which the data processing manager can make time and service allocations among potential users. Assignment of priorities for the limited time and services of the data processing organization among the competing user units is a problem plaguing every data processing group, regardless of its location or degree of centralization. This is not a function that the data processing manager can carry out effectively without some form of guidance to the entire organization from management. Whatever the form of these guidelines, and whether the emphasis is on long-term rather than short-term applications—sales analysis rather than payroll, accounting rather than marketing—such guidelines provide all members of the organization with an outline of management's expectations from computer applications. It then becomes the job of the data processing manager to interpret and administer the guidelines and allocate time and services in keeping with them. For the data processing manager to be placed in the position of gaining acceptance of his priority assignments by the manipulation of organizational relationships is a disservice to the data processing activity and to the units within the organization that seek to use the activity's services.

A Look to the Future

Running through the foregoing conclusions is the theme of the computer's applicability to management's needs and problems. Tremendous gains are in store in the ability of managers to narrow the range of uncertainties in the future, to choose more viable alternatives from a wider range, and to see more clearly the import of the most abstract and conceptual aspects of the enterprise. Computer-oriented information systems are largely responsible for this expanded range of management capabilties.

REALIZING EDP BENEFITS

Managements are better able to shape the organization to adapt to the rapidly changing requirements of the market and of other external factors which bear on the business. Such organizational configurations also can help to unleash the human creativity so urgently needed in this age. Again, the use of computers to support information systems will enhance the ability of organizations to mold and shape themselves to the form needed.

In many other ways, the concept of the computer-based information system indicates strides, which companies are beginning to take only now, in improving the art of management.

However, since information systems do not organize themselves, companies will share in the bounty offered by computerized informational techniques only if their managements take pains to see that the electronic data processing and information systems activities are located within the organization where they will be most effective in implementing a broad corporate approach to the development of the needed computer applications. As we have indicated, we believe this end can usually be accomplished through a separate data processing/information systems function reporting directly to top management.

Wherever it is decided to locate these activities, the decision is one that should claim the full participation of top management. Since the impact of computer technology, as applied to information systems, on the

traditional business organization may well be more pervasive than any other single technological, social, or political development on the horizon, it is too important a decision for the long-term future of any company to be made by data processing experts, organization specialists, or divisional managers.

TIME SHARING AND ITS IMPLICATIONS

While the decision to centralize or to decentralize the computer activity will be based on factors other than purely technological ones, the potential of time-sharing technology can be expected to play a significant role in how these decisions will be carried out.

Awareness of the benefits to be gained through a computer time-sharing capability have contributed significantly to the trend toward centralization and autonomy of the computer complex. Indeed, the centralization of the EDP operation on a significant basis probably would not be feasible without time sharing in some form.

So far, the uses of time sharing have tended to support the trend toward centralized computer operations. In the future, however, it is possible that extensive time sharing, involving the use of a central computer processing unit, linked with users by input/output terminals, may contribute to the decentralization of the EDP function.

Through time sharing, several hundred users can have simultaneous, or what appears to them to be simultaneous, access to one computer system. The actual time required to perform the computational steps of most programs, measured in milliseconds and picoseconds, has long been vastly ahead of the time required to feed information into the computer and to get the output. Thus, input for a single program is introduced laboriously—or relatively so—into the computer, which performs the computation in two or three milliseconds and then waits until the results have been displayed and new data have been received. This process entails tremendous waste in the heart of the computer system—the part that also is the most costly.

Within the past two or three years, significant technological steps have been taken to utilize this waste time. Using a series of buffers and storage control devices, a number of computer systems now are capable of accepting input from a number of sources, of processing the programs at once (or of working on one for a while and then swinging to another program before coming back to the original one), of quickly storing input data until free internal processing time is available, and of displaying output data in a variety of ways. To the user, the time lapse in these steps is so short that, in many instances, the computer's response to given input data seems instantaneous. From the user's point of view, the computer might just as well be dedicated to his exclusive use; he is unaware that perhaps another 50 to 100 programs are being processed at the same time as his. The computer's ability to deal immediately with a program—for example, change it in mid-process to correct errors which the computer has pointed out —also has added considerable flexibility to the process.

The use of time sharing clearly can affect the location of the computer activity within the organization. For one thing, outside service bureaus, which can provide shared time at a fraction of the cost entailed in tying up a whole computer for a single program, are attractive to those user organizations that experience difficulty in getting their programs on the company computer. Several units in the companies in this study have turned to outside service bureaus for this reason.

More important than the effect on location, however, is the thrust toward greater centralization of EDP activities, which is resulting from the capability for time sharing. Several of the study companies are endeavoring to bring together the bulk of EDP activities in their organizations by establishing service bureau facilities within the company. The intention is to encourage divisions having their own computer capability to use the corporate computer center in much the same way as they would use a service bureau. Thus the time-sharing concept becomes a reality—the central processing units for the entire corporation will come to be housed in such centers and will be surrounded by terminals at the various user organization locations. From the terminals, users will be able to talk directly to the central processing units in the computer center and will provide input data and receive output data. Most of the companies in this study, in the opinion of those interviewed, are headed in this direction.

Attempts at time sharing are still quite rudimentary in most companies. Experience among the study companies ranged all the way from those without any time-sharing capability to one company with such a high degree of time-sharing competence that it was considering the formation of a subsidiary company to act as an internal service bureau and to sell time to other companies. For the most part, however, actual use of time sharing lagged far behind the technical capability of the machines.

As is true of a number of technically feasible EDP advances, time sharing is not without its problems. Perhaps the major one is the extent to which it relies on communications devices. Most of the means of communications used, primarily telecommunications, still are quite costly, prohibitively so in many cases. Although some companies, such as public utilities and transportation companies, have reduced these costs by establishing their own systems, the lack of security in transmission of data, much of which are highly confidential and vital to any company's operation, poses still a further problem. In one utility company that has largely overcome the cost of communications by using its own radio and microwave network, which it had established for another purpose, the relative ease of data interception has caused executives to restrict the information that can be transmitted.

The eventual role of the Federal Government in regulating communications in EDP also will be a determinant of the extent to which time sharing becomes a broadly accepted and used device.

A system of outlying terminals and a central computer system also pose serious internal control problems. Who shall have access to the information in storage? Who shall have the authority to have programs processed on the central computer? How can unnecessary duplication of effort and expense be eliminated or avoided under such a system? By what method will costs of the central computer operation be allocated among the user organizations? How can plans for EDP activities be developed and coordinated if a user organization has an input/output terminal which enables it to undertake major EDP activity of its own on relatively short notice? These are some of the questions that must be considered in establishing internal controls under a time-sharing system.

There appears to be little question that time sharing or some similar concept will ultimately become very much a part of the standard EDP operating procedure. When this occurs, although it may not be for 10, 15, or 25 years, what will be the effect on the location and extent of EDP activity within the organization and on the assignment of responsibility for the computer complex?

Two major factors bear on this question. First, the extent to which a given company realizes the technical possibilities of time sharing will play a large part in determining changes in the location of the computer responsibility. A company that makes relatively little use of the computer's time-sharing capability may be faced with a considerably different set of determinations than the company that makes extensive use of time sharing.

Where time sharing is little used, considerable centralized control, either within divisions or within the company as a whole, of all aspects of EDP activity—systems design and development, programming and computer operations—probably will continue to exist. Obviously, such centralization would mean that the company would employ at least some time-sharing devices. Absent any extensive use of time sharing and the computer system itself and the activities related to it will tend to remain centered in the EDP organization, with user organizations coming to it for applications they want and for processing of their programs. On the other hand, greater use of time sharing will enable many of the elements of EDP to be pushed out to the user organizations. Under such conditions, the computer system can become the center of the operation, and systems development, operations research, and perhaps even programming become functions of user divisions.

The second factor that will help to determine the extent to which time sharing will affect the location of the responsibility for computer activities is the amount of knowledge and experience in EDP possessed by personnel in user organizations. As mentioned earlier, colleges and universities, secondary schools, and, to some extent, even elementary schools are devoting increasing amounts of time to instructing students in the theory and application of computers. When more of these students, trained in specialized areas such as marketing, personnel relations, chemical engineering, solid-state physics, metallurgy, and the like, and also solidly grounded in computer concepts, enter the company and begin to work in their own fields, the technical aspects of time sharing can be more effectively utilized.

In other words, when a company utilizes time-sharing technology and has a sufficient number of people in its various functions who are grounded in EDP, and as programming becomes more simplified, the company will be able both to create stronger EDP capability in the user organizations and to alter the scope of the activities of the centralized computer organization.

With extensive use of time sharing, responsibility for the corporate management information system may continue to center within a corporate staff unit, at least until such time as the computer can be programmed to provide the necessary coordination for the information system. Even then, there still may be need for a small central group to plan for revision and expansion of the information system.

Accordingly, the corporate staff group, probably a small unit of expert personnel, could conduct basic research related to computer applications; provide consultative services to user organizations on highly specialized points; and provide general coordination of EDP activities, as well as work on the broad corporate management information system, develop and modify the corporate conceptual model, and the like. Its function, under the conditions forecast here, would be to provide the necessary internal controls and conduct the basic EDP applications research that would be inappropriate to, or beyond the scope of, the user organizations.

Eventually, the computer system may be programmed to process the input from a division, display the output in the manner required by the division, and at the same time, process and store the input in a manner commensurate with the needs of a corporationwide information system. With such an arrangement, corporate managers could have their own terminals, with access to the corporate information system, and utilize them in making decisions based on a vast array of information in storage in different forms. Thus as information systems become more complete, and as computers are programmed to accept data from a variety of sources and assimilate them into a unified system, the need for intervention by a central information system staff group will diminish.

Under these conditions, operations research can be undertaken by the functional and operating divisions themselves, divisions which are most familiar with the problems to be solved. EDP-based systems can be developed and programmed in these divisions. Each user division may have and use its own input-output terminal for the development and processing of programs to attain its own objectives. The ancillary elements of EDP—operations research programing and the like—could become functions of the user organizations, and thus decentralized. The computer system itself could be used by these organizations for processing, in somewhat the same manner that mechanical calculating machines have been used for some purposes. Perhaps the only EDP activity that would continue to be centralized and devoted solely to EDP as an identifiable function would be the operation of the computer center. This would not call for the high level of managerial ability required by today's EDP activities in most companies.

This approach to EDP stresses its use for information purposes and the concept that the computer, after all, is merely a tool for management. Obviously, the approach to computer-based information systems and the location of responsibility for them envisioned here is not in the immediate offing in any company. As we mentioned before, because of the need to bring the level of computer knowledge, understanding, and experience in the workforce up to the level of computer technology, the approach set forth here may not come to pass for 10, 15, or even 25 years. Clearly, in some companies, it may never be adopted. But the growth of time-sharing technology, the increasing number of people trained in EDP as well as in their own specialties, and the continuing simplification of programming and programming language will make it possible for companies to follow this course in the future.

2. Location and Structure of the Computer Complex

In analyzing the location of the computer complex, it is necessary to distinguish between organizational location of the computer hardware and its related manpower resources and the organizational location of the responsibility and authority for directing the functions of the computer complex. In many companies the hardware, staff, and control reside in the organizational function; in others, however, several computer complexes (hardware and staff) are dispersed throughout the company at both corporate and divisional geographical locations, but the authority for management and coordination is at a single location at the corporate level or is shared by both corporate and divisional levels. Also, the location of the computer complex is always subject to change. Although the locations we describe in the study reflect the situation at a given time, they are continually being reviewed and shifted as company needs and objectives may dictate.

All the study companies have expanded the computer activity, and all have changed the location and reporting relationships of the computer complex. In this chapter, therefore, following a brief summary of the current organizational relationships in the study companies, we will examine the shifts in location and control that have taken place, as well as the major reasons underlying these changes in representative situations.

Current Assignment of the Computer Responsibility

In centralized companies today, management finds it fairly easy to organize computer operations as an independent function, since this reflects the company's organizational philosophy. The same approach is feasible, though perhaps more difficult, in decentralized companies. In the study companies, however, their managements have vested the responsibility in various organizational locations, even where there are such common characteristics of the companies as size, the existence of a general pattern of divisional autonomy (but with financial control encompassing the company), product diversity, and nationwide operational locations. In general, four patterns predominate in the companies for the assignment of responsibility for informational uses:

1. The authority for computer operations is centralized in a functional unit, ei-

EXHIBIT 1. *Assignment of Responsibility for the Computer Complex in the 16 Study Companies*

Company	Overall Style of Organization	Organization of Computer Complex	Location of Computer Complex Responsibility				
			Controller or Finance	Operations or Operations Services	Engineering	Other Functions	Independent Function
1	D	C-D	X				
2	D	C-D	X				
3	D	C-D	X				
4	D	D	X				
5	C	C	X		X^1		
6	D	C	X				
7	D	C		X			
8	D	C-D		X			
9	D	C-D		X			
10	D	C		X			
11	D	C					X (Reports to chairman or vice chairman of the board)
12	D	C					X (Reports to executive vice president)
13	D	D	X^2	X^2	X^2	X^2	X^2
14	D	C-D	X^3				X^3 (Reports to chairman or vice chairman)
15	D	D	X^4		X^1		
16	C	C	X^5				X^6 (Reports to president)

Key

C   = Centralized
D   = Decentralized
C-D = Both centralized and decentralized

1. Restricted almost exclusively to engineering applications.
2. Located here in some divisions, elsewhere in others.
3. Shared responsibility for computer-based information system between the controller and the data processing vice president, who reports to corporate top management.
4. Business systems; responsibility located here in divisions and at corporate level, but for business systems applications only.
5. Only for accounting systems; overall information system responsibility located in separate function.
6. Responsibility for overall EDP-based information system, except accounting system, which is under the controller.

ther (a) under the controller or an officer who has overall responsibility for the accounting function in the company, or (b) under another functional executive.

2. The authority is centralized in a top-level independent function.
3. The authority is divided over two or more areas, each of which has control over computer operations in its area.
4. There is no central authority for operations; this authority is dispersed among several divisions.

Exhibit 1 summarizes for the 16 study companies the current assignment of responsibility for information uses. It also illustrates the overall centralization or decentralization of the company as a whole and the degree of centralization or decentralization of computer operations.

As shown here, in 12 of the companies the responsibility for all computer operations, as they relate to management information uses, is clearly assigned to one location:

• Six companies report to the controller or to a manager who reports to the officer having overall responsibility for the accounting function in the company.
• In four companies the responsibility is assigned to functions other than ac-

counting. These are: operations services, which includes a number of services related to the company's operations but not accounting or finance; market research in a retailing company; operations in another retailing company; and a functional area with a wide range of diverse responsibilities in an insurance company. Each of these departments is headed by a vice president.

- In two of the companies studied, data processing, or information systems, exists in a single independent functional unit reporting to top management (the chairman, vice chairman, president, or executive vice president).

In the remaining companies the assignment for computer activities is less unified.

- In one of these companies there is no overall corporate data processing organization other than a staff function, and the computer complex reports to the controller in some of the divisions, to another function—engineering, operations, or research—in other divisions, and exists separately in still others.
- In a second company, the companywide information system—its development and content—is the responsibility of the vice president and treasurer, who reports to a group vice president, while data processing, as such, and the state of the art in the company are the responsibility of a data processing vice president, who reports to corporate top management. The data processing function is very closely related to the development of the EDP-based information system, since content and EDP technology are intertwined. Because of the duplication of these functions in the divisions and the amount of work already done by the divisions in these fields, the two departments coordinate in carrying out their joint responsibility.

- Another company's activity is divisionalized. Although it has a computer operation at the corporate level (in the treasurer's office), which handles some 50 percent of the company's total activity, the philosophy of divisional autonomy is so strong that each division has the authority to develop its own systems and to purchase or rent its own hardware if it wishes, virtually without any control from the corporate level. This company has a business systems corporate function reporting to a financial executive, but at least half of the data processing activity for information purposes takes place in the divisions, where it also reports to the business systems function of the controller's department.
- In the remaining company, responsibility for the broad EDP-based information system rests with a vice president who reports to corporate top management, but a significant amount of informational data processing activity is under the direction of the corporate controller.

These findings should not necessarily be compared with those of a 1965 study by the American Management Association[1] covering a larger number of companies, in which 70 percent of the survey companies showed EDP managers reporting to financial executives, while 30 percent of the EDP managers reported to nonfinancial executives. The difference in findings of the two studies may stem partly from the larger sample used by the AMA or from the size of the companies sampled.

In only six of the companies covered by our study is all, or the major portion, of

---

[1] M. Valliant Higginson, *Managing with EDP: A Look at the State of the Art,* Research Study No. 71, American Management Association, New York, 1965, pp. 34–35.

computer-based information systems activity lodged clearly in the financial or accounting function. In four companies, the responsibility clearly is assigned to functions other than accounting. Two companies have the EDP/information systems activity in a separate function reporting to top management. Responsibility for the function is less clearcut in the remaining four companies, but the patterns of responsibility assignment in these companies reflect a movement away from location of the responsibility in accounting.

This pattern in reporting relationships suggests that there is a trend among companies toward the creation of a data processing/information systems capability separate from the accounting or financial function. Where this separate capability exists, it reports to a top officer of the corporation.

As Exhibit 1 shows, the overall management approach in 14 of the companies is decentralization, but in varying degrees; the other two companies are centralized because of the nature of the company's business. Five of the decentralized companies, however, have centralized computer operations; six can be described as having a combination of centralized and decentralized computer operations; and three have divisional computer operations. Of the latter, two hold to a rather strict policy of decentralization in all operations—a policy that is reflected in the computer complex.

Since most of the companies are decentralized, and yet have either centralized computer operations or are moving toward centralization in computer operations, it would appear that a company's organizational philosophy need not directly affect its approach to the organization of computer operations. Moreover, as a subsequent discussion shows, even in those companies representing a firm commitment to decentralized computer operations, the emergence of some type of corporate control is evident, although at this time the authority centered at this control point is of course less than in the other companies.

Structure of the Computer Complex

How the computer complex is organized depends a great deal on where it is located, the degree of centralization of the overall company organization, and the extent to which the computer activity is moving toward centralization. The centralized computer complex in a highly centralized company has one look, reflecting the functions carried out by the EDP organization and, to a real extent, the absence of the need to sell a centralized approach to a group of doubting division managers. A centralized computer activity in a decentralized, divisionalized environment has other problems, other functions, and hence, another form of organization. The company with an effective EDP capability in the divisions, but moving toward greater corporate centralization so that several computer efforts—one corporate and the others divisional—exist side by side, organizes its computer complex still another way. Examples of the organization of the computer complex under each of these conditions are set forth below.

CENTRALIZED EDP FUNCTION IN A CENTRALIZED COMPANY

In one highly centralized company all of data processing, except for financial accounting, has been brought together into a data processing/information systems department (see Exhibit 2). This department is headed by a vice president who reports directly to the chief executive officer. The key function in the department, below that of the vice president, is that of systems analysis and programming. Although some sys-

EXHIBIT 2. *Example of Organization of a Centralized EDP Function in a Centralized Company*

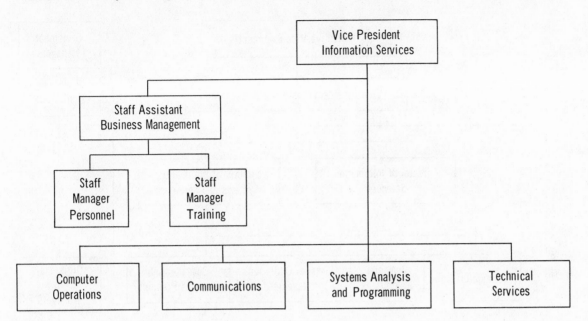

tems development capability exists in some functional departments, all of the systems development work in the company is done by this unit or under its close guidance.

The unit, in turn, includes 12 functional sections, each under a section manager, covering such activities as applications planning, applications programming, data-base programming, software design, and the like. An important coordinative function within this unit is that of documentation coordination. Responsibility for development of a model to be used in simulating the information system itself is also lodged within this unit.

Other units within the data processing and information systems department are computer operations; communications, including telecommunications; and technical services. The technical services manager serves as the liaison for the vendors, the users, and the technical facilities group within the department and works with them on the schedule and technical specifications for installation of hardware at the central site and at all remote locations. He also works with the hardware and software groups and with the department's communications people.

This company's data processing and information systems department is sizable, both in staffing and in its impact on the overall organization through the computer-based information system, solidly located in the department. An indication of the department's proportions is that it has its own business manager, who handles budgets and other administrative matters, its own personnel manager, and its own training manager.

The strength of this department stems from the fact that it is the data processing and information systems unit for the entire company. It is actually doing the work entailed in developing and operating a comprehensive computer-based information system rather than coordinating its activities with those of a number of divisions, as is true with most of the study companies. The EDP organization is in a favorable position to play this role, largely because it is a centralized operation, functioning under exec-

EXHIBIT 3. *Example of Organization of a Centralized EDP Function in a Decentralized Company*

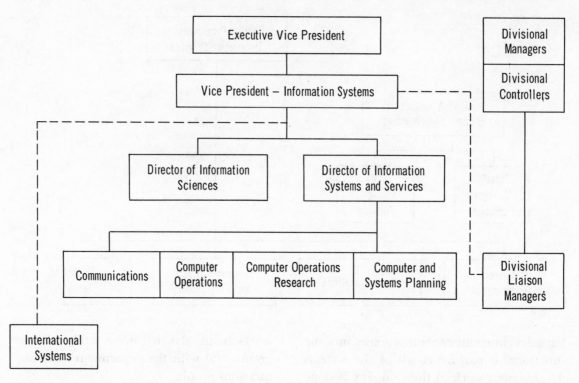

utive mandate, in a company whose executives are accustomed to operating in a highly centralized mode.

CENTRALIZED EDP FUNCTION IN A DECENTRALIZED COMPANY

This situation is handled in a variety of ways by the study companies, the primary variable being where the individual company is at a given point in time in its progress toward a highly centralized EDP activity. But the company that we will discuss provides an outstanding example of effective organization of the computer complex to deal with this delicate and difficult organizational problem.

In the sample company, which is endeavoring to increase the extent of its already highly divisionalized approach to management, most elements of the computer activity are completely centralized and have been

since 1954 (see Exhibit 3). The major exception to the centralized mode in EDP is systems development, since much of the work is done in the divisions in close cooperation with the central EDP group. The hardware and EDP personnel are all centrally located at corporate headquarters. Since the divisions also are headquartered in the corporate office building, the divisional liaison personnel are physically located near the central EDP group.

The corporate information services function is headed by a vice president who reports to the executive vice president. The function's head also serves as secretary to the company's operating committee. His department includes the information sciences and information systems and services. Under the latter are communciations, computer operations, computer operations research, and computer systems planning. Development and operation of international systems also reports to him, and the divisional liaison managers, who report directly to their division presidents, report to him on a functional basis.

This department is set up to operate the company's computer systems—to program and to work closely with the divisions in developing information applications—but the department clearly controls the overall EDP-based information system. The formal relationship with user divisions, through the liaison managers, is designed to ensure that divisional needs are recognized by divisional management and met by the corporate EDP organization, and that divisional applications coincide with the informational needs of the corporate system. It has proved to be an extremely effective organization for accomplishing these ends.

DECENTRALIZED COMPANY WITH BOTH CENTRALIZED AND DIVISIONALIZED EDP FUNCTIONS

Like most of the decentralized companies in which the direction of computer activities is evolving toward centralization, this sample company is gradually building up its central corporate computer capability while the established divisional computer operations continue to function. The objective of this approach is to centralize without the jarring impact of a reorganization from the top. Thus the centralized EDP group can demonstrate its ability to aid the divisions and, eventually, will come to be regarded as an in-house service bureau by user organizations, many of which will reduce their EDP capability and use the service bureau.

In this company, again as in most of the divisionalized study companies, a high degree of computer competence exists in the various divisions, both functional and operating. But recognizing the duplication that exists in the divisional EDP activities and

the need for a broader corporate information system, company management has determined to centralize EDP activities, and steps have been taken in this direction. At present, however, both a corporate capability and a divisional capability exist. As part of the centralization effort, all computer acquisitions within the company must be approved by the corporate EDP group, and all communications activity is guided by this group. Moreover, a substantial computer center, linked to various company locations by telecommunications, exists at corporate headquarters, and more and more divisions are using the center because it has more advanced facilities than most of the divisions could afford to support individually.

This organization of the computer complex points up the need for indirectly selling the divisions on using centralized EDP. In this respect, one of the most effective techniques has been for the corporate group to develop an effective system for a division, at its request, and then make sure that other divisions know of this, in the expectation that the system can be installed in other divisions.

As shown in Exhibit 4, the computer complex is headed by a director of management systems. Each of the functions reporting to him—divisional systems, information systems laboratory, equipment and communication, computer center, and systems and organization consulting—includes a group of consultants who are involved with corporate-level EDP developments but who also spend much of their time working with divisions on a consultative basis. This direct involvement with the divisions, in an attempt to demonstrate the capability and viability of the centralized EDP group, is reflected in the organizational make-up of the computer complex. The involvement is especially apparent in the divisional systems function in the department, which exists

EXHIBIT 4. *Example of Organization of Computer Complex in a Decentralized Company with Both Centralized and Decentralized EDP Functions*

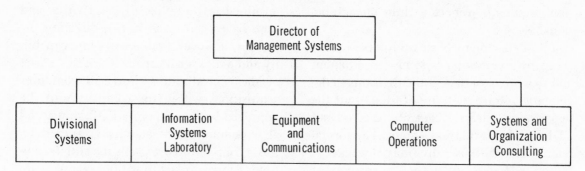

specifically to work with divisions in the development of their systems.

Factors Influencing Location

From company experience it is quite evident that careful study and analysis, which generally characterize top management's determination of the organizational structure needed to achieve its business objectives, frequently did not accompany the introduction of the early computers. As computer technology developed, however, and business organizations became more complex, it soon became apparent to the study companies' managements that the computer was a tool of great potential, but that often, because of the location of the computer's authority in the organization, its full capabilities were not being utilized.

EARLY COMPUTER LOCATIONS

The widely held view of the first computers was that they were immense calculating machines; accordingly, their initial use in most companies was in the accounting field. The charts of accounts in use to promote standardization and the quantitative nature of accounting seemed made to order for computers. Also, many managements decided not only that the computer was more suited to accounting work than to many other endeavors but that it seemed

less likely to disrupt the organization in this area. Thus many a controller in the 1950's and early 1960's fell heir to the responsibility for the new device, the computer. The early applications merely transferred the existing recorded data to the computer and computerized existing systems. The principal objectives were usually savings in clerical costs and more rapid data processing.

This was not always the case, of course. In some companies with strong research and development or engineering organizations, people in these functions were among the first to realize the possibilities of the computer. Consequently, in such companies, computers were introduced through the research or engineering departments.

One significant difference often emerged when the computer found its way into an organization under the auspices of a research or engineering department. Rarely did the research or engineering department manager make any serious attempt to become the focus of any proposed management information system, whereas this often did happen when the controller had initial responsibility.

Because the controller's function necessitates his cutting across divisional and functional lines, it was only natural for him to begin to examine ways of standardizing some aspects of accounting, and perhaps even other sources of management information, on a companywide basis to better feed his computer. As interest in management information systems broadened, especially at the upper levels of management, there came the need for someone in the company to be responsible for developing such a system. This usually fell to the controller, because most of the discussion on management information systems, in both management circles and in meetings of technicians, seemed to center around the use of the computer, and because computers tended to be the responsibility of controllers. Thus a growing number of controllers found themselves with the assignment of building and operating an information system for management.

Researchers and engineers, on the other hand, were largely interested in the computer as an aid to their research and engineering efforts, and the computer's application to the rest of the company tended to be of little moment. What the research and engineering managers did fight for, and what some still are fighting for, was a separate computer facility, complete with computer equipment and the skilled personnel to plan, program, and run it, to be devoted solely to research or engineering. As a result of such efforts, some companies (three in our study) have two sets of substantial EDP operations—one devoted to research or engineering applications and the other to the management information system. Often this duplication stems from the importance to the company of research or engineering. Sometimes, however, it exists because of the power of an individual research or engineering manager.

A Broadening View of the Computer

The early simplistic view of the computer and the absence of management attention and planning concerning its functioning led to unsatisfactory results for many companies, including the failure to realize antic-

ipated cost savings.[2] With the advent of the third-generation computers in the 1960's, however, came greater awareness of the computer's potential and a shift toward a more centralized operation of the computer complex. By this time data processing had gained acceptance in the area of its initial application, and EDP-based systems had been worked out for those applications. A number of companies, including several in this study, believed that they had developed their data processing capability and the competence of their information system beyond the point where either could be applied profitably only to purely accounting operations. Their experience with information systems, together with more advanced computer technology, raised questions about the validity of a computer location which permitted the responsibility for data processing and information systems to repose in the accounting area, or in the controller's office, or in any other established functional area.

As a result, many companies decided to move the responsibility from accounting or another functional area and to reassign it to a new functional vice president; more often, however, when the functions of data processing and information systems were moved, they were then grouped together, perhaps along with other related operations, into an independent organizational unit. In several of these instances the new unit reported directly to the chairman, the president, or to an executive vice president.

The Relocation Process

The length of time that a company has had a computer, the management's astuteness in recognizing the computer's poten-

---

[2] John T. Garrity, "Top Management and Computer Profits," *Harvard Business Review*, July-August 1963, pp. 6–8+.

tial, and the special demands made on the computer have all affected the extent to which the location of, and the responsibility for, the computer has been changed. Beyond this, there is an overriding factor which stimulates all managements to examine and relocate their computer operations—this is that the computer is (and will become more so in the future) a vital element in the company's ability to maintain and enhance its competitive position within its industry. While there are different levels of sophistication in computer usage in the study companies, the level of sophistication of companies within the same industry tends to be comparable because of the need to stay abreast of competitors.

As shown in Exhibit 5, all of the study companies have made some change in the location and control of the computer complex. Not only have varieties of changes occurred in the relocation process, but there is marked divergence in many companies between the original setting for the computer operation and the present setting, reflecting advances in computer technology as well as a deliberate decision by the company's management to gain better utilization of its computer equipment.

Basically, six general types of shift took place in the study companies during the relocation process—all but one resulting from management's planning for a more effective approach when it realized that the company was not getting full benefit from its computer.

In centralized organizational structures.

1. A shift of computer hardware and control from a number of functional units, all having their own computers, to centralization of computer hardware and control in a single location at the corporate level.

In decentralized organizational structures.

2. A shift of computer hardware and control from a number of divisional units to a centralized corporate unit having control over the complete computer complex.

3. A shift of some, but not all, computer hardware, staff, and control from divisional to corporate locations, with corporate and divisional (but predominately corporate) control of selected key functions, such as equipment purchase, cost review of programs, approvals, and so forth.

4. Continuation of divisional hardware and control, but establishment of a corporate computer complex to operate in an advisory role to the divisions and to seek coordination among the divisions on a voluntary basis.

5. The establishment of a corporate control and coordination function (excluding hardware) but with divisions still maintaining substantial autonomy over hardware, operation of the installation, staffing, and determination of programming.

6. Maintenance of divisional autonomy for computer complexes—but with one division acting as a service bureau for other divisions on a voluntary basis. (This centralization occurred not as a result of management's plan, but on an informal basis, as a result of one division's convincing other divisions that it would be to their advantage to use its "service bureau.")

All of the companies believe that these planned changes have resulted in more effective operations, not only by lowering costs and gaining more effective utilization of the computer, but by the development of more significant programs that will eventually contribute to a comprehensive management information system.

REASONS FOR CHANGES

In most of the companies, relocation was the result of a combination of factors. For

EXHIBIT 5. *Transition in Location of Responsibility for the Computer Complex*

Company	Originally – Located In	Originally – Responsible To	Currently – Located In	Currently – Responsible To
1	Divisions	General Managers	Corporate Headquarters Divisions	Vice President General Managers
2	Divisions	Engineering Controller	Corporate Headquarters Divisions	Controller Division Controller, Engineering
3	Divisions		Corporate Headquarters Divisions	Controller
4	Divisions		Corporate Headquarters Divisions	Treasurer Vice President, Administration
5	Accounting Division	Vice President, Finance	Accounting Division Engineering Division	Vice President, Finance Vice President, Engineering
6	Divisions	Division Controller	Corporate Headquarters	Controller
7	Corporate Tabulating	Controller	Corporate Headquarters	Vice President, Administration
8	Divisions	Operations Services	Corporate Headquarters Divisions	Vice President, Research Vice President, Operations
9	Divisions		Corporate Headquarters Divisions	Vice President, Operations Services Divisions Controller, Operations
10	Divisions		Corporate Headquarters	Vice President, Operations
11	Divisions	General Manager	Corporate Headquarters Divisions	Chairman General Manager
12	Divisions	General Manager	Corporate Headquarters	Executive Vice President
13	Divisions	Divisions Controller Divisions Operations, etc.	Divisions	Divisions Controller and Industrial Relations Operations Corporate Coordinator
14	Divisions	Mostly Division Controllers	Corporate Headquarters Corporate Headquarters Divisions	Controller Chairman of the Board Division Controllers
15	Accounting Division Engineering Division	Controller Engineering Controller	Accounting Division Engineering Division Divisions	Controller Division Controller Division Controllers
16	Divisions	Division Managers	Corporate Headquarters Accounting	President Controller

example, while one of the managements realized that its computer complex was not organizationally located or structured in the best way, it did not wish to disrupt the organization by making a change, and so it postponed action until more advanced computer hardware, which provided the rationale needed for a smoother transition, was acquired. In the future, continuing advances in computer capabilities and telecommunications will undoubtedly enable companies to time changes so that they can be made over a period of time against a projected goal.

Awareness on the part of management of the computer's potential for developing programs that cut across functional lines and benefit the entire company is the most perceptive reason for relocating the computer. Such foresight was evidenced by the top management of a decentralized retailing company, which recognized that the establishment of uncoordinated computer complexes in various functional and regional locations would set the future pattern for installation of computer operations in the company. While separate installations might serve the divisions well, this approach was considered inefficient and uneconomical for the company as a whole; thus the management felt that centralization would have to take place at some future time. Accordingly, it established one central computer complex with complete authority to determine what programs would be developed, their priorities and operating standards, and to select and train computer personnel. This determination was made almost at the outset of the company's first exposure to computers. Although only a few computers were acquired at this time, and they were used as tabulating machines in separate locations, no sooner had they been introduced than management foresaw their potential, made a thorough study of broad company applications, and quickly set up its centralized computer complex. Because the computer was not yet firmly entrenched anywhere in the company, it was easier for the management of this decentralized company to get acceptance for a centralized operation.

Relocation of the computer was the result of management planning in a number of other cases, but the planning was belated and came about after unsatisfactory experience which pointed up the need for a broad objective and a planned approach.

One of the study companies originally believed that since it was decentralized the best approach was to permit computers to be introduced in various regional locations. In the absence of any central coordination and direction, however, wide variations developed in the competence of the regional centers in using computers. Each region designed applications for its own needs; thus it became impossible for the corporate management to get an accurate, cohesive picture of operations throughout the company. In fact, results obtained by the computer system were less accurate and more costly than those which had been achieved by noncomputerized systems.

A third reason for changes in location and control was the top management's realization that while decentralized computer complexes were effectively serving divisional needs, no companywide programs were being developed. Most of the companies to which this applied permitted the division complexes to continue but established a central computer complex for program development. In addition, the central unit was given authority to review divisional programs and to ensure cost savings by (1) making certain that the programs being developed were significant, and (2) preventing duplication of functional applications among the divisions. The company foresaw the advent of advanced computers and wanted to be ready for the day when one centrally located, sophisticated computer could replace the divisional installations.

As noted earlier, the third-generation computer has enabled the management of some companies to put its plan for relocation into operation and to combine the effective elements of separate computer complexes into one central complex.

In one rather unique situation a company reorganized its computer operations in order to provide for a continuing advanced research capability. It supplemented its divisionalized computer complexes with a corporate computer unit that had responsibility for developing and maintaining day-to-day companywide management information systems. At the same time a separate computer section was set up to undertake advanced research and was free to direct its entire resources to programs for future company use.

Despite the various reasons that the companies had for relocating their computer complexes, two basic objectives underlie these changes:

1. Cost savings to the company as a whole, not only through more significant, specific applications, but through more effective utilization on a companywide basis of the corporate computer complex, including its hardware, manpower, and programming capability.

2. The development of new, advanced applications not associated with specific cost savings but directed toward areas of greater profitability.

EDP OBJECTIVES

Whatever the reason for change, in most of the study companies the planned relocation of the computer has resulted in a more effective operation. As previously noted, in the early stages of computer development the commonly held view of many managements was that the computer itself was only a mechanism for processing data to provide information for use in any of several operations—operating a refinery or pipeline, scheduling production line runs, directing a numerically controlled machine, calculating and preparing customers' bills, providing information for accounting and financial analysis, and so forth. As long as managements saw the computer in this light, there were no special problems. However, this view did not reflect any insight into the broad use of the computer in managing the business.

Among the study companies the impetus for relocation of the computer came when the top management gained a basic understanding of the computer's potential for serving the company as a whole. At this point they recognized that the EDP function—more than any other corporate function—could pervade the entire company organization, cutting across and interrelating organizational components, levels, and functions, and that this could be done without destroying the concept of decentralization. This view made it possible for top management to establish long-term objectives for the computer complex, objectives which were designed to achieve benefits for the entire organization. The setting of more precise objectives might be assigned to the central unit, if there were one, or it might remain the mutual obligation of division and corporate units working together and become an evolving process.

The broad objectives which management sought usually were: Should computer utilization be directed toward developing programs with broad companywide application and benefits, toward meeting the divisions' needs for certain applications, or toward serving a combination of the two? Within such objectives, the management might decide to reduce costs, to expand present uses (but without an increase in staff), to computerize existing systems to retrieve some information more quickly, or to re-trieve more and additional kinds of infor-mation which management could use in corporate decision making.

The determination and articulation of overall long-term objectives for EDP activi-ties must be, and in most of the study com-panies eventually have been, undertaken by top management. These objectives operated as major determinants of the location and direction of the computer complex.

But the setting of overall objectives only charts a course. The approach to following that course and the specific decisions and implementations that must be undertaken in the evolution of the computer as a factor within the company are determined else-where. In the study companies these deter-minations fell largely to the EDP organiza-tion. As a consequence, in those companies with both divisional and corporate EDP ac-tivities, considerable cooperation was re-quired between EDP people at these two levels. The evolution of the computer ac-tivity toward the objectives set by manage-ment is the result of a series of decisions made in this way and shaped largely by the individual company's specific situation.

One of the problems that has to be dealt with is that, within the same company, dif-fering objectives for EDP uses may exist, and these differences can lead to active con-flict or passive resistance to relocation of computer responsibility. To a marked de-gree, differences in views on what the ob-jectives should be reflect the functional ori-entation of the executives involved. In one study company, for example, the EDP ac-tivities were moving from a wholly division-alized operation to a consolidation of com-puter operations in selected subsidiary companies; these companies would then serve other subsidiaries. This process was being guided by a corporate data processing manager who played a large role in hard-ware acquisition and systems development.

Although the objective was considerably short of complete centralization, a move-ment toward greater centralization was evi-dent. Thus the plan met with strong disap-proval from a powerful vice president of administration in one of the major subsid-iary companies. His background was in ac-counting, a function which reported to him.

DECENTRALIZED OR CENTRALIZED EDP ACTIVITIES?

In the course of determining the basic EDP objectives, top management also de-cides, in line with corporate objectives, the level of authority to be delegated to the EDP function, the function's place in the organizational structure, and its relation-ship to other organizational units. In the study companies, the location has come to be regarded for the most part as a top man-agement decision, to be made on the basis of what positioning will be of greatest ben-efit to the company as a whole and at the same time will enable the computer com-plex, centrally or divisionally, to serve the needs of divisional and other organizational units.

Clearly, the corporate data processing manager in the sample illustration was guid-ing the company to increased EDP central-ization. His objectives were increased sav-ings, greater effectiveness of EDP operations throughout the company, and an informa-tion system that would link all of the inde-pendent subsidiary systems into one unified whole. And to do these things, he needed greater centralization.

In opposing the centralization tide, the subsidiary vice president was seeking quite different objectives. In his eyes the informa-tion aspects of the company's business be-longed in the accounting function. His ob-jective was to provide a staff function that would supply management with the ac-counting information it needed. He was dubious of the role the computer could play in achieving this objective. In fact, he saw in the centralization of the EDP/information systems activity a negation of the staff concept. In his words:

> Centralizing the hardware and its operation makes some sense. But there is nothing to be gained by centralizing or controlling software and systems planning. An operating manager has to know what form he wants information in before the computer can give it to him in usable form. With centralized systems development, he may get more information than he needs or can use. Under this centralized approach the EDP organization no longer is a staff group providing information. Instead, it becomes the master architect of what it wants done in the company.

The difference in objectives here is apparent. But top management in this company has concluded that the objectives are not quite as dichotomous as they appear, and it has decided to move toward a broader information system, requiring closer cooperation among the subsidiaries and, thus, closer guidance from the top. Management believes that this approach will further the objectives of the subsidiaries as well as those of the overall company.

The greater cost and increased capabilities of third-generation computers make centralization of EDP activities attractive to many managements on a variety of counts, as we have seen. Yet this attraction need not (and indeed does not in the study companies) dictate an automatic decision to centralize. In each study company the decision to centralize or decentralize computer operations was made by management in light of a specific situation in the individual company. To these managements there was nothing inherent in the nature of the computer and its uses which inevitably led to centralized EDP.

In most of the companies, neither the overall management philosophy nor the company's organizational structure unduly influenced organizational structure and relationships of the EDP operations. Though a company was decentralized and had a highly autonomous, profit-centered, divisional organization, the EDP organization was not decentralized merely to sustain consistency with the overall pattern of management organization and operations.

In those companies where the computer operation is working most effectively, the decision to centralize or to decentralize computer authority was based on the overall objective to be served by EDP activities, considered in the light of circumstances peculiar to the company—the diversity and complexity of its products, the geographical location of its organizational components, and companywide needs weighed against divisional needs and the present stage of computer development. Also considered were the current status of EDP operations in the company, the company's organizational structure and relationships, and the current and near-term state of the art in computer and telecommunications developments.

It is easy, perhaps, when the major part of a company's management functions and operations are centrally located, to determine that the computer operations, including the hardware, should be centrally organized and located. In decentralized companies, however, the decision is more difficult. Judging from the experience of the study companies, there is no predominant approach other than that dictated by the individual company's situation.

In actuality, in most of the study companies there was no true dichotomy of centralization or decentralization of computer operations, but a greater or lesser degree of centralization or decentralization. The important consideration, and the significant guideline for achieving computer effectiveness, was that the organization of computer operations, whether centralized or decentralized, was planned on the basis of management's needs, and that there was a centralized corporate computer function to coordinate overall companywide computer operations.

Significant Trends

Two trends in the location of the computer complex are discernible at the present time. One, the trend toward greater centralization of computer activity and of responsibility for computer-based information systems, is quite strong and appears to be bringing rapid change within business organizations. The other trend, toward the creation of separate and independent data processing and information systems activity reporting to top management, is not as strong and does not portend as rapid a change. It is, however, a clearly apparent trend at this time.

Only two of the companies in this study operate in a highly centralized mode, and this is dictated by the nature of their businesses. The remainder are decentralized to varying degrees. Yet all but three of the companies surveyed have centralized all or most of their data processing activities that relate to information systems or are in the process of doing so. Two other companies have, or are considering, regional computer facilities to tie together divisional activities. Thus the trend toward a central grouping of computer activities, usually at the corporate level, is strong and appears to be gathering momentum.

TREND TOWARD CENTRALIZATION

Among the primary reasons for the movement toward EDP centralization were the following three, all of which are closely interrelated.

Increasing management demands for companywide information. As the size and complexity of operations increased, the need for prompt and comprehensive information about all of the company's operations for management's use in directing the enterprise also increased. More and more companies learned they could not afford the luxury of operating in a totally or highly decentralized mode when information systems were involved. Too much potential, in the form of needed information, was lost when each division went its own way. Information obtained by one division sometimes yielded little or nothing to corporate management and often duplicated information being gathered and processed by another division. Or divisions accumulated similiar batches of information but processed them in such a way that they were useless for corporate analysis purposes.

Even though a particular divisional computer application might not yield anything essential to corporate management, there was no reason why the division should not make use of the application; however, the pressure of growing informational needs of top management led corporate EDP staffs to attempt to standardize divisional systems and programs so that, should a need arise for the information in the future, it would be available in a form that would not require reprogramming or the design of a new system to obtain it. Moreover, this growing pressure made EDP managers increasingly aware of the urgency and value of creating a data base within their companies upon which to build their ever widening information systems.

The absence of a comprehensive data base and the difficulties of creating one are major impediments to more effective information systems in most companies today. Compatibility among systems and programs in divisional operations is essential to the establishment of an adequate data base for the whole corporation. It has become increasingly evident to the managers to whom we talked in the course of this study that the only way to obtain this configuration is to repose greater authority and control in the corporate data processing function.

Cost factor. This was found to be closely related to the increasing demand for companywide information. Not only could companies not afford the luxury of a number of independent, self-contained systems from an information-gathering point of view, but many could not afford it from a purely economic standpoint. The sight of divisions, each with its own third-generation computer and EDP department developing and running the same programs and obtaining the same information as other divisions, while each computer was actually in operation only 15 percent of the possible time, was a painful one, not only to the corporate EDP manager, but also to the financial officer and to top management.

The introduction of third-generation computers having greater flexibility and capacity than their predecessors pointed up the growing need for EDP flexibility within companies because of the varied nature of the systems being developed. Given the cost of the new computer systems, a division, acting totally on its own, would have to decide whether to acquire a third-generation computer and the needed flexibility along with it, even though the capacity of the system might far exceed the division's demands (and considerable, expensive idle time would result), or to forgo the flexibility on the grounds that it could not afford the third-generation computer.

This oversimplified, but illustrative, dilemma is one that has added impetus to the trend toward centralized computer facilities. Managements in companies that decided in favor of central computer facilities reasoned that the divisions could not share the cost of third-generation computers and

the personnel needed to program and design for them without sacrificing flexibility. With the central computer facility serving as a service bureau, each division could use the computers to the extent necessary without incurring the cost of an advanced but underutilized computer of its own.

Shortage of EDP personnel. This continues to be an extremely difficult problem for all EDP operations. The supply of trained computer personnel, especially top systems people, has fallen behind the demand for their skills. Moreover, as we will discuss in a subsequent chapter, our study companies found that the time needed by a company to train its own EDP personnel became a burden on the ongoing EDP operation. In an effort to pool the EDP personnel resources in the company and to get the maximum benefit from their services, some companies combined the EDP groups of several divisions, establishing group or regional EDP centers, or brought all possible EDP personnel into the corporate organization. Indeed, one EDP manager in a highly decentralized company told us that if the computer activity became completely centralized in his company, it would be because of the shortage of computer personnel and for no other reason.

INDEPENDENT STATUS OF THE COMPUTER FUNCTION

The actuality of data processing and information systems as independent, separate functions, combined for the most part, would appear to be somewhat far off for most companies. Yet our findings lead us to believe that such a trend does exist currently. The number of companies that have undertaken such a shift recently, combined with the number that are working in this direction, are significant enough to constitute a trend. Several of the data processing managers interviewed reported that the identification of their activity as one with independent status stemmed from increased interest on the part of management in the computer and how it could be used to obtain more companywide information.

Many, probably most, of the writers in the field of computers and management conclude that, overall, the most effective location of the computer activity is in a separate department, either on a par with other functional departments, such as marketing, accounting, and manufacturing, or as a staff department reporting to top management. But as a number of these writers point out, and as our study confirms, a separate and distinct computer activity may not be appropriate for every company. Indeed, in some companies such an approach could be disastrous. (In a few companies, including at least one in this study, it actually has been.) In those companies, management support and understanding of EDP uses are limited and, therefore, management's view of computer uses is restricted to specific functional areas, such as accounting, or marketing or sales analysis. Early in the development of computer informational uses,

a separate EDP/information systems function would not be geared to the operation expected of it by management and would tend to be less effective than if it were located within the functional area with which it was most closely identified.

Of much greater importance to the decision of where to locate the computer complex than the theoretical "ideal" location are such considerations as:

- The traditional style and philosophy of management in the company.
- The "state of the art" within the company—how long computers have been in use, the extent of EDP capability within the company, the size and adequacy of the data base on which the computer can work, the acceptance of the computer as a management tool by company executives.
- The need for computer applications, and the extent to which such applications are required on a companywide, cross-functional basis.
- The availability of competent leadership to head up the computer complex wherever it is located.

3. Orienting the Computer Complex To the Total Organization

Closely related to the organizational location of the computer complex are the responsibilities of those in the EDP organization and their authority to carry out these responsibilities. Moreover, in the companies included in this study, the nature of these responsibilities and the part they play in the achievement of EDP objectives are affected in large measure by where the computer activity is located within the organization. For example, in one company with two EDP networks, one centered in the accounting function and the other created to provide a broad management information system, the nature and extent of the authority and responsibilities of the two organizations are quite different. As the vice president, information services, of this company describes the situation:

> Although the first uses of EDP equipment were in the accounting area, as early as 1931 in some cases, we found out about two years ago, through an economic evaluation of other potential uses for the computer, that there was gold to be mined in broader areas than strictly accounting or order applications. So we set up the information services department and drew the line between it and financial accounting, which now has its own EDP organizations reporting to the controller. We could have drawn the line between real-time processing and batch processing just as well, because that's the way the two departments and their operations have worked out.

As a result of this reorganization, the information services department in this company now has responsibility for all EDP activities except those which are purely operational and those which are under the controller's office. The decision to separate the financial accounting use of the computer from other EDP activities carried with it real restrictions and limitations on the authority and responsibilities of the controller, with respect to new or expanded uses of EDP. Although one can only speculate about alternatives, it seems clear that had the decision been to place the entire corporate EDP activity under the controller and to expand his scope, his responsibilities—and his authority with respect to EDP —would have been much broader than they are under the present arrangement.

In the companies in our study the responsibilities of the EDP managers went far beyond direction of the specific functional operations of the computer complex. Most of them were acutely aware of the need to integrate their activities with the existing organizational structure. We found that in a number of traditionally decentralized companies, the EDP staff at corporate headquarters was extremely careful to avoid doing anything that would lend credence to the belief, held in some functional areas or operating divisions, that the company was gradually being centralized through means of the computer. Consequently, their major challenge was to win broader acceptance of their function and to gear the overall computer approach to both corporate and divisional objectives. Concern for success in these efforts was expressed by practically all of the EDP managers to whom we spoke. Their approaches and some of the problems they encountered are described in this chapter.

Achieving Common Viewpoints Toward EDP

There is a significant lack of understanding between company managements and EDP groups in many companies. Members of some EDP organizations tend to be more interested in what applications can be developed for the computer than in what applications actually are needed by users, and what guidance these users need in order to utilize the computer more effectively. Line and staff managers, on the other hand, often are reluctant to give up old ways of doing things in order to adapt to the standardization required by the computers. Many tend to regard computers and EDP people with suspicion. Or on the basis of the experiences of other companies, they sometimes make excessive demands on their own EDP organizations. Also, some managements have placed restrictions on the EDP group that have resulted in underutilization of facilities. Such problems stem from a lack of real understanding and support of the EDP operation on the part of both management and EDP groups.

One of the responsibilities, then, that the computer organization shares with company management is to attempt to bring about greater mutual understanding between the two. So far, on the basis of the experience of the study companies, the major efforts have been in terms of "educating" management and have consisted largely of encouraging managers to use the computer more by increasing their understanding of what it can do.

ORIENTING MANAGEMENT TO THE EDP FUNCTION

Clearly, attitudes toward the computer held by top management, by middle managers, and by the employees themselves have their effect on the data processing organization and its ability to function. Among employees these reactions vary greatly and are related somewhat to the employees' degree of proximity to the machine. In a study of the changes in attitude by psychiatric-hospital employees toward their computer, named "Bertha," Drs. Donnelly and Houck observe that: "Computer interaction with individuals is very like the interactions of individuals with one another."[1]

Similar phenomena were found in the course of our study. For example, a typical initial response of a middle manager when approached about a possible computer application was, "What can that machine do for me that I'm not already doing better?" With the exception of a few die-hard resisters, the almost inevitable reversal in attitude changed the above response to, "I need more information on all of these things. Why can't you put them all on the computer now?"

---

[1] John Donnelly and John H. Houck, "The Personality of the Computer—How It Grows and What It Does," address before the 123rd annual meeting of the American Psychiatric Association, Cobo Hall, Detroit, Michigan, May 11, 1967.

In this connection, the story is told in one of the study companies of a marketing vice president who, enthralled by the vast possibilities of the computer for gathering information, overrode the objections of the EDP people and demanded a massive body of data. On the appointed day, the printout was delivered on three hand trucks, loaded to capacity. This illustration, although an extreme case, points up the demands which may be placed on the EDP operation by users whose enthusiasm for information outstrips their knowledge of what data are actually needed.

The change in attitude, from wanting nothing to do with the computer to impatience when large quantities of computerized information are not made immediately available, is so typical that it can be charted. The stage in the metamorphosis when a middle manager calls for more and more data, only to find himself buried under a deluge of unusable figures and reports, places a strain on the data processing organization and may turn the manager of the user unit against the use of the computer for his operation, at least temporarily.

Recognizing this fact of organizational life, each of the data processing managers participating in this study considers among his duties the education of other people in his company to the potential uses of the computer. Some do so in a rather superficial, haphazard manner, while others have developed elaborate courses similar to those run by equipment vendors and have sent a steady flow of company executives and other employees through their programs. A divisional data processing manager in one company announced that when a substantial change was made in the computer equipment and in its applications to the division's operations, he had run everybody in the division, from the president to the secretaries, through a training course to educate them as to what was involved. Thus

the need to educate their fellow company employees about the computer is felt keenly by data processing executives.

EDUCATIONAL PROGRAMS FOR LINE MANAGEMENT

Every computer group in the study companies had held computer training courses for one or more levels of management. These programs varied greatly, from a single one-afternoon presentation to intensive in-depth sessions. Some were conducted by the vendors and some by the companies themselves. Several of the larger EDP groups developed capsule versions of vendors' training programs, which geared the course content to the company involved. These courses also saved training time and prevented overemphasis on the equipment of a particular vendor.

At one time, EDP managers generally believed that line managers should attend schools or courses conducted by the vendors, and most of the study companies still depend on them for much of their computer educational programs. Such courses, which are usually from three to six days long, are most frequently conducted at the vendor's location, requiring the participant to be absent from his job. At least one vendor, however, will send a training man from one of its regional offices into a company to conduct an all-day course or a series of afternoon training sessions. In general, those EDP managers who have used these courses concede that, in the absence of a tailor-made program of their own, the courses conducted by vendors provide the best training available. But they do not feel that these courses are the long-term solution to the problem of educating management to EDP. They point out that, by necessity, the vendor's course material must be related to what the computer can do in general rather than to the problems of a specific company. One executive vice president reported that a vendor's representative who conducted a training session for executives in the company's offices had tried to assimilate enough about the company to relate his material to problems that would be recognized by the group, but his efforts were not successful. Moreover, the emphasis which the vendor naturally places on his own computers during the training courses is a limiting factor in the eyes of most EDP managers. They believe that this tends to give the participants an unbalanced view of the EDP field.

To overcome such shortcomings, the EDP organizations in several of the study companies have tried several approaches. One company has had success in using both vendors' representatives and consultants from a university computer center. EDP people and non-EDP executives who have participated agree that the results have been good. From this, a continuing relationship is being maintained among EDP people in the company and at the university. This keeps university people abreast of computer developments in the company so that they can help develop training material.

Another company, also working with a university, has developed its own intensive computer concepts program. The team of instructors for each course, which is one-and-one-half days long, consists of one man from the university and one man from the company EDP group. Participation is limited to 12 executives at one time. Company EDP people state that they have condensed a manufacturer's course of six days into one-and-one-half days and have added some additional material in such areas as identification of problems to which EDP is applicable, systems design, and the outlook for the future of EDP. Response from company executives has been enthusiastic. So convinced are the EDP manager and his staff—and corporate management as well—

of the effectiveness of the program that the company now admits course participants from other companies, mostly customers.

But these are merely the mechanics of bringing a greater knowledge of EDP to the line manager or staff man. All that can really be done is to spark an interest in the subject and show the ways in which EDP can be of assistance to the executive. In fact, this is all that most EDP managers expect from such short training programs. They realize that the real "education" of the executive will take place only over an extended period of time, with the continued demonstration of what the computer can do for him.

For this reason much of the educational work in EDP, as in any function in business, is done on a low-key, informal, personal, day-to-day basis. Typically, the data processing manager keeps himself informed about developments in a particular function where he believes that computer applications may be possible. At each opportunity he points out these applications to the manager involved and attempts to explain how the computer could assist in the operation of the department.

Thus the formal training course approach is aimed at creating a climate of general understanding and appreciation of the computer and its capabilities throughout the company; educating or selling an executive in terms of a computer application for his own operation tends to be much more pointed and less formal.

INCREASING LINE MANAGERS' PARTICIPATION

Although the computer is being used increasingly, most managers have yet to realize its vast potential as a management tool. Many still see computer applications as mere replacements for existing systems or procedures and as devices to process data more economically or more rapidly.

This failure to be more innovative with the computer may be attributed in part to the fact that line managers have a less-than-complete grasp of the computer's capabilities and also fear that the computer will strip them of some of their prerogatives. In addition, they sometimes regard the determination and development of computer applications as solely the province of a central or divisional computer organization.

The gap is narrowing through efforts of EDP managers, such as the educational programs described above. However, the greatest impetus to full line management utilization of the computer undoubtedly comes from endorsement by a top management that fully comprehends the computer's possibilities as a management tool. This was illustrated again and again in the study companies—sometimes quite dramatically. For example, the president of one of the companies had, at one time, headed the original computer study; and, as president, he made it clear that he expected broader use of the computer. This was communicated throughout the company by his emphasis on divisional cost reduction objectives. Also, he established a staff group, reporting to him, to uncover areas having companywide potential for cost reduction, and to determine their adaptability to computer applications. As a result, the managers in the company who had resisted EDP applications to their own operations or who had been cool to the EDP concept were placed in the position of having to look to the computer as a tool that would help them reduce costs in line with the president's mandate.

In another company, management assigned to one man, who was tremendously interested in the computer and fascinated with its potentialities, responsibility for a study of the company's overall computer needs. Although he became executive vice president shortly after the EDP study was launched, he continued to explore the computer field and even received programming training. All of his colleagues were very much aware not only of his grasp of computer technology, but of his understanding of the computer's capabilities and of his belief that all managers should be familiar with the computer and make use of it. His example, because of his prominence within the organization, had a marked effect on the attitudes of others and was largely responsible for the success of EDP operations in his company.

Aside from educational programs, the approach toward involving managers of user units in the process of developing systems applications and in determining future applications is probably one of the most crucial factors in gaining management acceptance of the EDP function. One very effective method used by a number of the study companies to encourage line management to use the computer more fully is to maintain a close relationship with divisional user organizations. In one company this relationship is maintained through special personnel which act as liaison between each division and the EDP group. These liaison men represent their divisions in all computer activity. The most effective men have both a comprehensive knowledge of their own divisional needs and the ability to acquire knowledge of computer technology and operations. They not only offer the insight needed for determining areas that will benefit most from computer applications, but also can identify the best sources—whether individuals or reports—of information needed in developing functional applications. In this company the liaison function is a formally established one and reports within each division. Other companies less formally assign relationships with particular divisions to members of the EDP staff in order to enable them to become familiar with the specific problems of a limited number of divisions and line managers.

Two advantages are gained from orienting line management in this way: (1) The line person contributes constructively to development of computer applications; and (2) through his direct involvement in the computer organization, he sees firsthand how the computer can be used by those alert to its capabilities.

In addition, there is a third advantage to the liaison approach. The computer function serves as a planned training assignment for line managers because of the broad view of the company operation which can be gained by learning of other company functions through work with computer operations. After the liaison person is advanced to a more responsible position, he not only has a broader view of the management function, but is able, through firsthand knowledge, to demonstrate the advantages of the computer to his own unit and to promote the value of computer technology to other line and staff management personnel.

Also to encourage greater line management participation, central computer units in several of the study companies have adopted a policy of conducting feasibility studies of potential applications and preparing cost-and-saving estimates at no or little charge to the potential user. Some also make special promotional efforts to sell line management on the computer's ability to increase efficiency and cut costs in specific operations. In a sense this has required the EDP organization's guarantee that an application would prove beneficial to the line user and that all deadlines would be met.

ORIENTING THE EDP STAFF TO COMPANY NEEDS

Because it is not uncommon that they lack the perspective of the overall company organization, members of EDP organizations, as we have noted, often believe that the authority of the EDP group should be greater than it is in order to require the other functions to cooperate more fully in providing data. They also often believe the EDP group should have a freer hand in determining the order of new EDP applications and establishing priorities for the development of these applications.

In general, these specialists have not performed in other functions, and while they comprehend fully the intricacies of the computer, the actual functioning of the overall company organization, as such, either does not interest them or confuses and frustrates them. They clearly see the vast potential of the computer for their companies and frequently become impatient with organizational restrictions that impede their progress toward realization of its potential.

Thus EDP managers are confronted with the problem of orienting their own staffs to management's needs. And though not so common as the programs aimed at educating management, more programs are being directed to the education of EDP personnel in the problems and objectives of the managements of their companies.

EDP managers are usually concerned with the need for encouraging junior men in EDP to realize that their work is an integral, but not necessarily controlling, part of the total effort of the organization. Toward this end, several of the computer organization managers to whom we talked are planning courses to better acquaint their people with the management point of view. One of the study companies, for example, has asked the corporate personnel department to set up a training program for EDP people that will feature a series of presentations made by executives and specialists from every company division and department. These executives and specialists consult with the manager of EDP to determine which of their department's activities will be most meaningful in the training sessions, and they then shape their presentations to show how their operation fits into the total organization.

Others have attacked this problem, as we have seen, by closely relating the activities of one individual or group within the computer complex to a particular department or function. Such EDP departments are composed, in part, of groups which specialize in bringing the computer to bear on the activities of specific functions, such as accounting, research and development, and marketing. Each group restricts its work to one functional area so that the members of the group—some EDP specialists and some experienced in the particular functional area—become very familiar with the needs and problems of their area of responsibility and with ways the computer can be used to overcome them.

The use of line people in liaison positions, as discussed earlier, also helps to indoctrinate EDP personnel to the company, as well as to bridge the gap between line functions and the EDP operation.

Leadership for the EDP Function

In a number of the companies studied, the caliber of the individual charged with the EDP responsibility was reported to be as important, or nearly so, as the functional needs of the company or division. Ideally, these companies seek an outstanding man, already working within the function in which the major need for systems or data processing exists, who can establish a separate function. But failing this, they may turn to another function where there is such an individual and assign computer responsibility to him. One of the criteria

against which men in the latter category are gauged is their ability to adapt to a situation in which they will be devoting most of their time (at least initially) to solving problems of another functional manager through applications of the computer. Overall, the ability that is most widely sought in the manager of a data processing and information systems function is a combination of flexibility and a broad view of the company's needs and operations. Capability of the individual is the paramount selection factor in one company in which the computer responsibility resides solely in its divisions. Whether the computer operation in these divisions reports to a scientist, a controller, or what, it still *depends upon the individual.*

Because computers are relatively new, at least in their more sophisticated applications, few top-level managers have both broad company experience and a thorough grounding in computer technology. What has emerged in recent years is that an executive, who has 10 to 15 years of experience in company operations, has become interested in computers and their application to his company and has applied computer technology to his areas of responsibility. Through a combination of computer training courses, reading, and work with the computer, the operating manager/computer expert in almost every company covered in our survey managed to accumulate considerable proficiency in computer techniques and applications. Only one of the EDP managers with whom we talked is primarily a bona fide computer expert with outside experience, rather than a manager who has supplemented his knowledge of the company with training in computers.

This method of obtaining the necessary combination of company experience and computer training is not limited to top-level executives. It holds just as true for managers one or two levels below the top data processing/information systems executive; relatively, they also are late-comers to computer science. At the lower EDP supervisory levels the majority of persons have spent their entire business careers exclusively in the computer field.

Unfortunately, few EDP specialists in the study companies have devoted sufficient time to acquiring knowledge of general company operations. EDP people appear to have been primarily occupied in keeping on top of their rapidly expanding speciality, and this tendency has made it difficult to select EDP managers. As one team of researchers has observed, "Companies tend to put operating people in charge of the computer because it is believed easier to educate them about computers than it is to teach systems specialists about a business."[2]

Several home-grown data processing/information systems managers predicted that the problem of combining general company knowledge with computer knowledge will continue to plague most companies until those individuals who have had early training in both computer technology and other phases of business operations begin to rise to higher levels in the company. The point these managers are making is that no matter how much information and knowledge a man gains about a subject in his 30's, 40's, or 50's, that subject will never be as comfortable for him, nor will he use it as naturally, as the knowledge gained in his formative school years. However, young men are beginning to come into companies today who have been trained in marketing, personnel work, accounting, and engineering, and who are also capable of designing systems, programming, and operating computers. According to one recruiter of engineering graduates, "You find scarcely an

engineering graduate today who can use a slide rule, but they all know how to run a computer." This is, of course, somewhat of an exaggeration, but it points to the fact that a generation has grown up with the computer and to them it seems like the most natural of tools. Out of the ranks of this generation will come the managers of tomorrow.

Achieving Compatibility of Divisional and Corporate Objectives

Companies in our sample vary in their approach to control of data processing, from highly centralized to highly decentralized. Seven companies fall into the highly centralized category. In six of these the entire computer capability of the company, with minor exceptions, is located geographically and organizationally at corporate headquarters; access to the computers themselves and to EDP personnel may be had only through various forms of input/output devices and terminals. At the other extreme, two companies surveyed do not have a computer at the corporate headquarters and have only small staffs of EDP people; all of the data processing and actual information systems work is done in the field by the divisions, which have their own hardware and their own EDP/information systems staffs.

Within this broad range, it is interesting that the highly centralized computer organizations are quite conscious of the role of the divisions, and that the EDP staffs in the highly decentralized companies have endeavored to put the corporate imprint on as many of the broader aspects of divisional activities as they can. Even in those companies with tight central control over data processing, if there is a difference of opinion between a particular division and the corporate staff over whether to accept

[2] James W. Taylor and Neal J. Dean, "Managing to Manage the Computer," *Harvard Business Review*, September-October 1966, p. 103.

or to reject a proposed new EDP application for that division, the decision rests, as a practical matter, with the division's management. In each of the study companies, the corporate EDP staff is acutely aware of this situation and attempts to sell the divisions on new applications long before the decision-making point is reached.

Thus in even the most centralized EDP organizations there are elements of decentralization when the company's overall operating mode is one of decentralization. Similarly, there are elements of centralization in the highly decentralized approach to computer control. For example, in one company so decentralized, the corporate staff reviews proposed expenditures by the divisions for computer equipment, both rentals and purchases. Its coordination of the development of major EDP projects is based on persuading divisions to cooperate in interdivisional exchanges of experience and programs and to attain companywide configuration of their systems. The director of data processing in the company describes his role this way:

My staff is made up of computer experts. Our job is to aid the divisions in setting up their programs, to set up meetings of EDP people in the divisions, and generally to pass along information and encourage the exchange of information. Also, I try to get the divisions to accept new ideas, but I try to keep them from undertaking something they don't need. Any computer-related expense request for anything more than $10,000 a year gets reviewed by me. But if there is an honest difference of opinion between the division management and me over whether something they want is a need or merely a frill, the division manager prevails. But differences are rare, and when they occur, the argument usually does not lie with the division manager, but is a question of lack of understanding. I find that the fact that someone is looking over the divisions' shoulders on this makes them right in their judgments more often than they would be without that check. For example, some 95 percent of the equipment requests are not arguable in any way.

In all of the companies surveyed, therefore, there is a strong trend toward increased centralization of the EDP and information systems, resulting primarily from a desire to realize more of the benefits available from computerization. For the person in charge of the computer complex in a company moving toward centralization of EDP, the question of how to encourage the user divisions to use the central facility in such a way that functional or divisional EDP objectives and corporate EDP objectives blend into a consistent relationship poses real problems.

COMPANIES MOVING TOWARD CENTRALIZED EDP

In those companies where computers came in through one or more functional or operating divisions, and where they have been in use in these divisions long enough for substantial skill to have been attained, computer objectives tend to be closely oriented to the needs and applications of the individual division. Several of these companies now are centralizing computer operations. During the transitional process the divisions generally continue to pursue their goals, while the task of the central computer group is to attain a degree of compatibility between the divisional objectives and uses of the computer and the broader objectives that the company is striving to reach through consolidation. In most of these instances the approach of the central computer group is to require corporate-level approval of the divisions' new computer applications to ensure that they contribute, at least in part, to the overall corporate objectives, and to prevail upon the divisions to modify any existing systems which do not conform to corporate goals. In general, the central computer organizations seek to encourage the development of those divisional applications and the establishment of those divisional objectives which will contribute to overall corporate objectives as well as to divisional operating efficiency and profitability.

The scope and focus of divisional aims in the study companies are related to the degree of centralization of computer activities. In those companies with strong and effective central computer activities, the divisional goals are, or are becoming, narrower than they have been in the past. But even in those companies with no truly centralized computer capability, steps are being taken to secure divisional adherence to corporate standards and objectives, which will enable the corporation to evolve a broader information system. In one of the companies with no computer capability at the corporate level, for example, the corporate EDP staff is able to combine some systems for use among several divisions, to pass on proposed computer acquisitions, and to guide the divisions fairly closely in developing computer applications with the eventual corporate goal in mind.

Despite close controls from the corporate level, the divisions can exercise considerable latitude in the establishment of their objectives. Among the study companies this was true particularly of profit-center divisions, which reflected the decision-making authority inherent in their organizations. While these divisions conformed and directed their EDP efforts to support corporate EDP objectives, they still could determine and select the EDP applications which they needed in their operations.

The reconciliation of divisional objectives with central objectives was well illustrated in three of the study companies, each

of which followed a different approach to achieve the same goal—that of establishing a broad, overall corporate information system.

In the first company all computer activities are centralized except for some phases of systems development and input/output editing and control. Although divisional management is free to determine the applications needed to improve divisional operations, the systems are developed under the direction of the central EDP staff so as to generate information that can be used directly by the chairman, the president of the company, and the top management group. It is not unusual, therefore, to find that one division's application is a model of its total operations which, while it contributes to the divisional objective of cost savings, has as its primary objective clarification of the interdependencies of various operations to facilitate planning and direction of the total organization. Another division may have developed, as a cost-saving objective, an application for more effectively pricing raw material, as well as an application for achieving an optimum end product as a quality control objective. A third division may focus its EDP effort on better marketing analysis and forecasting. All, however, are designed so as to yield important data to top levels of the corporate organization.

In the second company the relative autonomy of the divisions is strengthened by the fact that EDP sections existed in each of the divisions before a centralized EDP operation was established. In this company, corporate objectives serve as guides, but the varying needs and services of the divisions underlie independent divisional objectives. All three of the company's divisions support cost savings as the general corporate goal. The division that initiated computer operations in the company, however, has already developed its primary cost-savings applicaplication and has revised its objective, which is the development of innovative aplications which will yield broader services.

The third company relies on liaison personnel, who represent such functional groups as accounting, research and development, and marketing, but who are attached to the centralized EDP operations, to influence divisions in developing their EDP operations and to bring about greater consistency in interdivisional objectives. In addition, the centralization of divisional EDP operations within the divisional controller function tends to bring divisional and corporate EDP objectives more closely together.

It is apparent from our study that although EDP operations may be highly decentralized, they are directed toward autonomous divisional objectives; thus it may be difficult to establish mutual goals among the divisions, or goals for divisions and the corporate operation, that are compatible. Nonetheless, all but one of the corporate EDP staffs in these companies are trying to attain greater compatibility. Some companies, of course, have experienced greater success than others in reconciling corporate and divisional aims.

DIVISIONAL DECENTRALIZATION OF EDP

In another group of three study companies, EDP operations, including computer hardware and EDP personnel, are decentralized on a divisional basis. All three corporate managements accept the principle of divisional autonomy and, thus, the primacy of divisional objectives on how the computer should be used. However, the relationship of these divisional objectives to those of the corporation differs among the companies.

In the first company the autonomy of divisional EDP operations is virtually unchallenged, and divisional objectives are only implicitly related to corporate goals. While the divisions evidence little interest in relating their objectives to corporate objectives, the corporate EDP operation attempts to involve the divisional EDP operations in the development of an information system, or series of systems, to generate more information for top management. As part of this effort, company top management recently strengthened the corporate EDP organization by increasing its size and upgrading its staff. The corporate EDP manager is working to develop closer relationships between the divisions' managements and their EDP organizations. In at least one instance he recommended the reorganization of one divisional EDP organization and recruited the individual who now heads it. In the main, corporate efforts to attain a degree of mutuality between divisional and corporate objectives have consisted of working with one or another of the divisions in developing systems which can also be used in the other divisions. For a variety of reasons, including the strong sense of independence that pervades the organization and the limited success of several of the model systems, these efforts have borne little fruit so far.

A strong corporate philosophy and tradition of operating highly autonomous divisional units, in which each divisional manager is held closely accountable for its success or failure but has a free hand to run the division, permeates the second company. This concept of organization is reflected in the autonomy enjoyed by divisional EDP organizations, both in their operations and in their objectives. Each division establishes its own objectives in the light of its own needs and operations, and many currently have quite advanced computer applications in operation. Two conditions exist in this company, however, which foster compatible divisional and corporate objectives. At the corporate level, a substantial computer capability exists in the controller's department, which, in effect, is the corporation's computer-based information system function.

That divisional and corporate goals are being brought together is evidenced by the fact that a number of autonomous organizational units have centralized their EDP operations within the corporate controller's computer operation. It is underscored also by the location of the computer complex under the accounting and control function in the divisions. Managers of these units are functionally responsible to the corporate controller and, therefore, are responsive to guidance from that office. Thus, in these ways, increased compatibility of objectives can be achieved through exercise of the corporate controller's influence on the divisional accounting and control managers, who direct EDP activities in the divisions, and through increasing divisional acceptance of the central EDP function under the corporate controller.

In the third company the dovetailing of corporate and divisional objectives has come about through the establishment of a corporate EDP coordinator function. This function recognizes the authority of the divisions in establishing their own objectives but, at the same time, exercises a fair degree of coordination and control to reconcile, more fully, divisional and corporate objectives as a prelude to greater centralization of EDP activities in the years ahead. The corporate EDP staff believes that a more consolidated body of information, derived from the company's diverse operations, will be needed in the future, and is now moving to obtain it. This staff has been able to develop increased cooperation among divisions in using hardware and in developing systems, and, through guidance and counsel regarding advanced techniques and hardware technology, has made the divisions more aware of corporate goals. Although this company probably is a long way from

obtaining, or even pressing for, divisional adherence to a set of firm corporate EDP objectives, it is moving in the direction of greater consistency in divisional objectives, which can pave the way for eventual acceptance of corporate objectives.

LOCATION OF EDP IN A FUNCTIONAL UNIT

Functional location of the computer complex is also a source of discrepancies between the objectives of the unit that has the computer and those of the corporation. When the corporate objectives to be achieved through computer use are essentially the same as those of the function in which the computer complex is located, there is no danger of conflict. Variances arise when corporate objectives broaden, as they have in most of the study companies, and the computer remains in a functional unit and is geared to that unit's operations.

In one company, for example, the computer complex was directed by a vice president of administration who possessed a strong accounting background and who was convinced of the applicability of the computer to accounting operations, since a number of effective computer uses had been developed in that area. When the company's chairman directed that work begin on the development of a broad computer-based information system, this vice president could not see the need for, or the applicability of, the computer to this endeavor, and since the development of the information system fell within his responsibility, he was able to restrict the adoption of new programming language, definitions, proposed applications, and standards, so that literally nothing but accounting data could be prepared for computer processing. Progress bogged down until the executive retired, at which point the EDP/information system activity was reorganized and placed under the direction of an EDP manager skilled in using the computer for informational purposes. Since the new EDP manager had worked closely with top management in a staff capacity in determining the overall objectives of the new information system, discrepancies in objectives were eliminated, and the whole organization began to work toward the same ends.

Similar situations involving resistance by the functional unit to corporate objectives have been dealt with in other ways. One company organized the data processing operation so that the desired broad-gauged information system became the responsibility of one executive, while the accounting systems already in effect, and the computer capability necessary to continue them, were left with the controller. The data processing manager reports directly to the president and operates a highly centralized computer organization, so there is little problem with maintaining consistency in objectives.

In still other companies in the study where the computer complex is part of the controller's responsibilities, the controller's function has been reorganized in order to reconcile functional and corporate objectives. Under a typical reorganization for this reason, the controller took on much of the business planning activity which, by its very nature, must be undertaken in furtherance of corporate objectives.

However, some of the study companies needed to have a major portion of the computer's use devoted to the needs of the functional division to which the computer was assigned. Their approach was to pursue divisional objectives in such a way as to have computer applications also contribute to the attainment of corporate goals.

For most of the companies in this study, which are moving toward centralized EDP, the basic consideration has been to keep the divisions' autonomy for determining and achieving their objectives, as dictated by their needs, in balance with corporate objectives and needs. This requires, first, establishing and communicating informal corporate objectives and showing their relationship to divisional objectives and, second, delegating authority to a corporate unit to coordinate divisional and corporate objectives and to make sure that they are the same. Within this context, the corporate EDP objective of most of the study companies, where feasible, is to develop computer applications which are directed toward building a companywide management information system. Although part of a division's objective is to contribute to the development of corporate systems, it may also have separate, autonomous goals which relate to specific and independent divisional needs.

4. The Computer Complex in Operation

THE EXTENT TO WHICH COM-
puter activities are centralized and their location have considerable bearing on the
functions carried out by the computer complexes in the study companies and on the
breadth of the computer applications that
are developed. In some, a highly centralized
computer operation performs all EDP activities. In a decentralized operation, the divisions carry out all such activities, and the
corporate staff merely provides guidance
and some degree of coordination and control. Moreover, part of the EDP activity,
such as systems development, may be located
in one functional area, while the responsibility for, and operation of, the hardware
and the actual programming may be carried out elsewhere, perhaps in a separate
computer complex.

Functional Operations

The categories into which most computer organization responsibilities fall include: acquiring hardware, operating the
computer installation, programming, designing and developing systems, assigning
priorities for new applications of the computer, selecting and training EDP personnel, identifying future projects, and developing managers within the EDP function.

Each function will be discussed in terms

of the responsibilities involved. Illustrative
statements on the responsibilities of a number of data processing organizations are
included in Appendix I.

ACQUIRING HARDWARE

Basic to any effort to achieve coordination
of EDP activities throughout the company
is control over hardware acquisition by the
various organizational units. The type of
hardware acquired largely determines the
scope and nature of applications developed.

In every company we surveyed, the corporate EDP staff, or some person at the corporate level, is involved in decisions on the
acquisition of computer equipment, either
through capital expenditure or rental, anywhere in the company. Usually, there is a
policy requiring that the corporate data
processing manager review proposed acquisitions above a certain amount. Even in
those study companies in which the divisions act independently in the computer
field, the purchase or lease of major computer equipment is subject to some, although slight, central control. In one company, approval for purchase or lease of
major computer equipment by the divisions
is secured by the same method and through
the same channels as approval for other capital expenditures, but an advisory committee, composed of representatives of the

ten largest divisional users, has been formed to serve as a clearinghouse for information on the capability and potential of new hardware and to discourage proposed purchases or rentals that might be inappropriate for the division concerned.

Typical of the policies that guide the corporate EDP manager in reviewing computer acquisitions is this one, adopted in mid-1966 in a divisionalized company that was moving toward tighter central control of its computer activities:

> With respect to equipment, this policy covers computer systems, tabulating equipment, and peripheral components, such as plotters and data communications equipment. The policy applies to all new or replacement equipment proposed for installation and having a monthly rental of $1,250 or more or a capital asset value of $50,000 or more.

Another company has established the review point at $10,000 a year. In a third company, in which subsidiary companies operate two major computer installations, the corporate data processing staff functions as an advisory and resource group to the subsidiary companies and has been charged with the following responsibility:

> To insure compatibility and avoid duplication, [the staff is to] provide advice and guidance to managements of the computer centers and to the subsidiaries on all proposals for ordering hardware to be installed both in the centers and at terminal locations.

In all of the companies surveyed, there is some corporate coordination of decisions to acquire hardware, and in nearly all, these decisions are controlled at the corporate level. Moreover, as computers' capacity and versatility increase, and as business information systems are designed to gather ever increasing amounts of necessary informa-

tion, divisions and subsidiary companies will be expected to contribute more and more information to these corporate systems and to the data bases upon which they rest. Since long-term plans concerning the relationships between divisions or subsidiary companies and projected systems are made at the corporate level—not in the divisions or subsidiaries—corporate staffs will probably weigh future plans of the subsidiaries for hardware purchases or rentals even more carefully in order to see how they would relate to a companywide information system.

There already is considerable evidence among the companies in this study that the trend toward centralization of the EDP activity has led to greater corporate staff control of hardware acquisition. The establishment of procedures for corporate review of divisional hardware plans often is the harbinger of further moves to centralize EDP activities.

OPERATING THE COMPUTER EQUIPMENT

The responsibility for operating the computer installation is quite clearcut in the companies studied. In one of these companies, there are no computers at the headquarters locations; EDP operations are the responsibility of the data processing organizations within each division. In one company, computer centers located in two of the subsidiary companies serve the business system needs of the remaining subsidiaries and of the corporate headquarters itself. In these subsidiaries, the manager of electronic data processing, reporting to a vice president of administration of the subsidiary company, is responsible for running the computer center.

On the other hand, in the companies in which all of the business system EDP capability is, or is becoming, centrally located, the head of the data processing/information systems function is charged with the operation of the computer facility. The corporate data processing managers also direct the operation of the computer centers in those companies that have established central computer centers to act eventually as service bureaus for divisions that now have their own computers.

Again, the strong trend toward centralized data processing indicates that, more and more, actual computer operation will become the responsibility of the corporate data processing/information systems organizations.

PROGRAMMING

With few exceptions, the programming function in the study companies is the responsibility of the individual who is also responsible for computer equipment operations. Very infrequently do systems people in user divisions or departments program their own projects. In those instances where they do, the divisional people continue to report to their division or department managers but work so closely with the EDP center group that they informally become members of that group. As a result of daily, almost continuous, contact with the EDP staff, the staff members of the user unit learn enough about the programming procedure followed in the computer center to be able to design programs ready for processing on the computer. However, a programmer attached to the computer center generally reviews a program laid out by a user division systems man, as a double check on whether it is ready for the machine.

Because the process of debugging is essential in programming, the programming function not only is located in the computer center but is often immediately next to the computer room or just across the hall from it. Also, because of the close relationship between systems development and programming, those performing these functions are situated in the same area. Often, of course, the systems developers are part of the computer center staff and do the programming of a system as part of developing it.

A definite trend toward blending the systems development and programming functions, so that they are performed by a single person, is evident today. Most company EDP managers prefer the combined capability, but people with both of these skills are in exceedingly short supply.

Since a system is a model of a dynamic reality, it must be maintained or altered when necessary to reflect changes in "the universe" on which it is based. Therefore, systems maintenance is another programming-related function that is performed in the computer center and that requires programming personnel, preferably systems-programmers. In one study company with a highly centralized EDP capability serving a number of product divisions, the computer center has to assign approximately one full-time systems programmer to each system, once it has become operative, simply to maintain it. Since this individual usually is a member of the team that originally developed the system, the maintenance function creates a heavy drain on an already scarce supply of systems-programmers at the computer center. Other EDP managers also reported a shortage of systems-programmer personnel because of the need to assign some of them to systems maintenance.

There was one exception in the study companies to the standard procedure of assigning all of the programming to programmers in the computer center. In this company, several operating vice presidents acquired an interest in the applications of EDP through the courses sponsored by the information systems division and, on their own, learned to use a relatively simple programming language. Thus they can program the information systems that they want processed. Programmers in the computer center then check these programs to make sure that they are acceptable to the computer. The executives' performance has been excellent. Initially, the EDP group was somewhat skeptical, but according to the head of the information systems division:

Although [they] were quite apprehensive at first, they now feel quite relaxed about it. We feel that it's probably very good for top executives to understand programming and what's involved in what we do. At least, these executives should understand such techniques as linear programming and what is involved in putting these programs on the computers.

DESIGNING AND DEVELOPING SYSTEMS

Whether or not the computer facilities are under corporate jurisdiction, EDP staffs at corporate headquaters encourage the divisions to develop and maintain their own capability for systems design. This approach stems partly from the awareness that a division-designed system will probably be more suitable to the division's needs than one created at headquarters, and partly from the divisions' concern with relieving the EDP personnel shortages which plague many centralized operations.

Four approaches to the location of the responsibility for systems work were apparent in the study companies:

- Putting the responsibility completely within the EDP/information systems organization.
- Putting it completely within the user divisions.
- Putting it in neither of the two but blending responsibility between the user divisions and the EDP organization.
- Establishing an independent corporate function to work with user divisions.

By far the most common practice is to assign systems design and development to the EDP/information systems function. This is as true of divisionalized companies, where the actual data processing function is carried out by the divisions, as it is of more centralized organizations. Where systems development is the responsibility of functional divisions within subsidiary companies, teams in each functional unit may develop the systems.

If responsibility for systems work is borne jointly by user divisions and the central data processing/information systems group, responsibility for developing systems usually is assigned to individuals in the user divisions. Their offices, however, are generally not located in their own division but in the data processing/information systems area, thus indicating the close relationship between the systems people, or divisional liaison men, and the corporate information systems division.

The divisional liaison man continues to report to his division manager; this helps to further the division's interest in the application of EDP-based systems. At the same time, through continuing contact with the computer group, the division man gains greater understanding of potential computer uses and problems that the EDP staff encounters in meeting the needs of all divisions.

When there is a systems development group at the corporate level, and similar groups within divisions that are not users of the corporate EDP services, actual responsibility for systems design and development may become blurred. There is no problem when it is understood within the company that systems for both division and corporate management use will be developed by corporate EDP/information systems personnel or that divisional EDP/information systems groups will create their own systems. But if more standardization of systems is needed, the responsibility of the divisional systems people changes somewhat.

In all but one of the study companies the corporate staff was expected, as a means of attaining systems standardization, to review, counsel, advise, and innovate, and to work with divisions having their own EDP systems capability. This somewhat narrows the scope of the division's responsibility for systems design and development, for although the division people can work up their own systems, this is done only within the framework of corporatewide standards. Also, the design aspects of divisional systems work are removed to a higher level. Responsibility for systems development remains much as it was, but since development exists only to implement the design, it can be argued that this aspect of systems work also has been altered.

From the standpoint of corporate versus divisional control, the locus of responsibility for systems design and development tends to be with the corporate or central group. Even in the one company in which the functional divisions of subsidiaries form their own systems, overall advice and guidance are provided by a small corporate staff of EDP experts. Since two subsidiary companies will be processing the systems for all other subsidiaries, it is imperative that all systems conform to the same pattern; only a group that supersedes divisional lines can provide the necessary interdivisional coordination. The corporate EDP group does this and, at the same time, inculcates the divisional systems people with the need to adhere to standards that permit effective functioning of a corporatewide information system.

Only one company permits the divisions clearly and absolutely to design and develop systems of their own choosing, without coordination from the corporate level. This relationship fits the needs and management mode of this company very well, but it is unique among the 16 companies studied. In the remainder of the companies, the corporate EDP/information systems group plays some part—either controlling, coordinating, or advising—in designing and developing business systems throughout the company.

ASSIGNING PRIORITIES

Regardless of the organizational location of the computer complex, all EDP managers are faced with constantly recurring priority problems. Each has only a limited amount of time on a certain number of computers to make available to company users and a limited supply of trained personnel to prepare systems and program them for users. Corporate EDP managers have more users to contend with, and they may be more powerful within the company, but divisional EDP managers in companies without a central computer complex face the same problems with user departments or functions within their own divisions.

During the initial stages of introducing EDP into most of the study companies, the managers of the data processing activity usually faced the task of convincing potential users of the efficacy of computer applications to their operations. Once this had been accomplished, however, the task changed. As managers of user organizations began to see how they might use EDP and computer-based information systems, they wanted to forge ahead and develop programs immediately. At this point in the computer's evolution within the company, the typical EDP manager had to attempt to allocate his resources, in terms of equipment, time, and personnel, among the users; to varying degrees, the computer complex managers in the companies covered here still are struggling with this phase of the problem.

Because of the typical EDP manager's location within the organizational structure of the company, the problem of priorities is not one which he can handle on his own.

Top management must provide general guidelines for assigning priorities among competing users. When top management issues such guidelines and supports them, the EDP manager is in a much stronger position to deal with competing users and is better able to prevent his resources from becoming so overburdened that applications are pushed through prematurely or from being squandered on relatively meaningless applications. While it is the EDP manager who must interpret and carry out the management's objective, the existence of a policy statement on EDP equipment and personnel utilization for users helps the EDP manager balance the needs of all users with his ability to meet those needs.

The problem of scarce resources and almost unlimited demand for them underlies the view that the data processing function should not be placed within any existing functional area. Those who support this position argue that, since resources are scarce, the functional manager who has the computer will utilize these resources to meet his own needs first. Then if there is anything left over, he will try to provide service to other functional areas. But some of the functional managers who oppose having the computer placed in some other area of responsibility are not completely averse to taking on the assignment themselves.

Establishing the computer and the computer-based information system as a separate function in no way eliminates the priority problem. Adherents of the independent EDP organization realize this. But, they contend, locating the computer complex outside the boundaries of any other function will help to ensure that all potential users get fair treatment when they try to obtain computer applications for their units. If computer facilities are limited, it may not be possible for the independent computer unit to provide users all the services desired; however, the existence of an independent unit does reduce the risk that certain users will get everything while others wait year after year for EDP services.

How priorities are to be assigned and handled is among the most critical issues in considering where the computer complex should be located within the organization. This question will be covered in greater detail later on.

SELECTING AND TRAINING EDP PERSONNEL

The shortage of skilled professional and technical manpower is particularly acute in the computer area today, and there is little relief in sight. The demand for competent computer personnel is so great that it is a relatively simple matter for computer personnel at any job level to leave one company for a more responsible job, or a similar job at a higher salary, in another company. Thus an important factor in an EDP organization's success is its ability to recruit competent personnel to staff it. In most of the study companies the personnel department was responsible for employing keypunch operators and other lower-level EDP positions. A number of the EDP managers, however, have worked with their personnel departments in developing tests for screening applicants and establishing standards.

The EDP organization plays a more prominent role in selecting employees for higher positions. Here the corporate or divisional personnel department is responsible for recruiting applicants through the standard avenues—advertisements, employment agencies, technical schools, and the like—just as it is for other positions. But interviewing and hiring are the responsibilities of the EDP organization, often the manager. Procedures here generally differ little from those used in recruiting scientific and technical employees elsewhere in the company.

In-company training of personnel is more important in the EDP organization than in most of the other functions in the company because of the difficulty of recruiting skilled EDP people; thus, training within the unit becomes essential. Moreover, many companies wish to staff the EDP function with employees having a company background as well as with those having outside experience.

Of course, the selection, training, and assignment of computer personnel are more easily coordinated and controlled in companies with highly centralized operations. In three of the study companies so centralized, all responsible management positions in the computer operations have been filled by individuals with considerable company experience. The companies make a considerable effort to recruit personnel from within the company and, in so doing, attempt to have all functional operations represented within the computer department. Each company regards the computer activity as an ideal developmental environment for management trainees; the work not only gives them a broad exposure to company operations, but helps to build a systematic approach to dealing with problems.

Few data processing groups are large enough to warrant the formation of a training section devoted entirely to training future programmers, systems people, and operators. More typically, training is done on the job by the regular EDP staff and is supplemented by some formal instruction and written material. This approach consumes up to half the time of the regular EDP staff in some instances.

In the study companies using this training approach, the idea is to develop broad-gauged generalists having both systems and programming skills. While the training period is fairly long and requires staff guidance, it is believed that the final result will be a more competent and versatile organization in which employee turnover is lower because each individual has an interesting

and challenging job with an opportunity to develop his capabilities further. After training, personnel from the computer unit are assigned to various functional programs.

A contrasting approach is followed in a fourth company, which focuses on developing specialists. This type of training can be accomplished more rapidly, and the breakdown into specialties tends to make responsibility for each function more clearcut and definable. The company believes this approach is more valuable because it makes it easier to spot omissions and weaknesses in a program before it is fully developed.

Each specialist is assigned to a specific functional area. Thus he becomes thoroughly familiar with the operations of the user and can develop programs more quickly. This approach, however, does not encourage flexibility in the computer unit, and the termination of a key functional specialist presents a difficult problem of replacement and training.

IDENTIFYING FUTURE PROJECTS

The uses of the computer in business and industry today represent only a fraction of those that are possible. No one is more aware of this than the EDP managers with whom we spoke. They are, in fact, the interface between the company as a whole and the EDP function. It is they who should best know the company and its computer needs, as well as the capabilities of the data processing organization. Thus they are in the best—perhaps the only—position to plan for future applications of the computer within their companies.

Plans for the future may entail relatively straightforward extensions of existing applications; they may contemplate the extension of computer applications into entirely new functional areas; or, as has frequently happened over the past two or three years, they may call for the conversion of the EDP operation from one type of computer system to a completely different one.

Although the part played by the EDP manager in planning for the future of his department may be relatively clearcut, his place in the implementation of such plans is not always as sharply defined. In *Managing with EDP: A Look at the State of the Art,* the 1965 AMA study referred to earlier, it was stated that in 80 percent of the reporting companies top management executives were the ones "who decided the major functions or projects for which computers [were] used in their firms." This conclusion was based on responses to a questionnaire sent to a cross section of management, from chief executives down, but with controllers and EDP managers predominating.[1]

In spite of such evidence, our findings indicate considerably greater participation by EDP managers in decisions governing future projects and functions for the computer complex than appeared to be the case among the companies studied by Mrs. Higginson. In a major petróleum company, for example, an assistant controller is known in the company, by middle and top management alike, as "Mr. Computer," and it is clear that his boss and members of top management look to him for guidance on the future path of the computer in their organization. In two other companies the presidents play an active role in determining future uses for the computer. The backgrounds of both men are, however, different from the majority of company presidents in that each has been active in the EDP organization of his company at some earlier point in his career. In fact, one of these presidents has been, to a large extent, the "Mr. Computer" of his company. But even he leans heavily on the vice president who has direct responsibility for the data processing/information systems function.

Computer technology is such a new field and is changing so rapidly that it is unrealistic to expect that any executive will be able to plan future computer projects unless he has had actual EDP experience. Even then, knowledge of the field rapidly becomes dated as he loses immediate, continuing contact with it. For this reason, many of the EDP managers in this survey stated that it is essential for EDP to report to an executive who firmly believes in it and who has the stature within the company to support it.

Of course, the actual decision-making process in determining future projects is much the same as elsewhere in the company: The EDP organization proposes and management disposes. Certainly, no assistant controller is going to make a decision that affects other functional areas and may cost thousands of dollars without securing the approval of his superiors. For all practical purposes, however, the decision to pursue a specific future project or function generally belongs to the individual in charge of the computer complex, who may be the vice president of information systems, the assistant controller, or the controller. This is the case in all of the study companies. Top management's decision is whether to approve a particular decision and the steps necessary to implement it or to reject it and, perhaps, to suggest other areas for the computer group's consideration. It appears to be rather rare for top management to initiate specific projects on its own. In fact, the only such instance we encountered, aside from examples in the two companies with EDP-experienced presidents, had failed and had been abandoned prior to our study.

DEVELOPING MANAGERS WITHIN THE EDP FUNCTION

Not many companies have taken real action in the development of EDP manage-

---

[1] Higginson, *op. cit.,* p. 35.

ment as yet, possibly because their computer complexes are relatively small. A few multidivisional companies with both centralized and divisionalized computer operations, however, are facing the problem of developing future EDP supervisors and managers. In addition, there are the problems of developing managers within EDP who can move to other functional areas with the benefit of firsthand experience in the computer field. The head of data processing research at one company told us:

> There is growing evidence of management concern over how to use the computer. It is a management tool that is growing in importance, and general managers have to learn how to handle it. Now, the management information systems sought by management really are the result of a drive to solve specific problems.

Another EDP executive stated:

> One of our biggest problems is to develop the man in the systems manager position in the division to the point where he can move up to the level of controller on the division manager's staff. This is more difficult, basically, than the question of the reporting relationship between systems and the controller. But the reporting relationship contributes to the problem sometimes, because it's hard for the systems manager to get the experience he needs to move up while he's developing and maintaining the systems.

To reiterate, very few companies appear to be doing much in EDP management development. The few EDP organizations now taking steps to develop their own managerial talent use rather elementary techniques since the organization is small enough to permit simple identification of organizational needs and of potential candidates to fill them. But as computer organizations grow and information systems become more far-flung, the need for planned man-

agement development within the EDP/information systems function will become increasingly apparent.

A food processing company has had success in meeting the problem of developing EDP people for higher positions in the organization. In this company the men who served earlier as liaisons between their divisions and the EDP department have later had a remarkably uniform record of promotions. The liaison relationship developed during the first phase of using the computer in the company, at which time a great deal of emphasis was placed on the computer's operational aspects. Nearly all of the liaison men in this early group have advanced in their divisional organizations, usually to the position of divisional controller, but in some cases to divisional vice president or divisional president. At present, however, the advancement problem again confronts the company, as much of the current EDP effort is in the area of model building; but because this work is being done in other areas of the company, the liaison men have not been greatly involved in it. Thus, partly because of a shift in the focus of the EDP activity, and partly because of the men involved, those in the early group of liaison men fared better, as far as promotions go, than those in later groups, who, for the most part, made lateral changes rather than advances. The potential problem which this may present is being watched by the EDP manager and the organizational planning people.

One of the retailing companies has also made effective use of its computer operations for developing management personnel marked for advancement. While the selection of user-liaison people was based on their ability to translate the needs and systems of the user organization to the computer technicians, it soon became apparent that the position enabled the liaison personnel not only to become technically proficient in computer usage, but also to envision significant applications to their functional operations. At the present time, therefore, the user-liaison function is maintained as a training position for individuals who are slated for promotion within their functional operations. The individuals who have been promoted have used their training to bring about significant improvements in their new locations.

Uses of the Computer

In the study companies the computer was introduced at the outset largely on the basis of the cost savings that could be realized, but as managements began to learn more about how the computer could be used, and as skills in using it were acquired, these companies gradually abandoned cost savings as the primary criterion. Though cost is still a factor—each of the benefits expected from an application is weighed against the cost of obtaining it—the basis for the computer's acceptance is no longer how many clerks can be replaced or how many dollars can be saved by doing a project on the computer. For one thing, the applications where cost savings can be readily realized and measured now are operational in many companies. Of greater importance, the computer is coming to be regarded as an aid to managing rather than as a powerful machine that performs traditional operations much faster and more accurately than can existing personnel.

After a brief review of some representative applications found in the study companies, this chapter considers some of the implications of future uses of the computer.

REPRESENTATIVE APPLICATIONS

Finance and accounting. Because the first computers were introduced in these func-

tions, it is not surprising to find the most widespread use of computers in these areas in the study companies. In most, the routine of designing accounting and financial applications has already been completed, and efforts are now being directed to more sophisticated analyses.

Computerization of accounting and financial data has revolutionized accounting and finance practices. The routine of collecting and preparing the data for reports, which was formerly a large part of the accounting job, is now accomplished by the computer, using basic source documents and initial reports. Thus the accountant has become more of an analyst, dealing with interpretation of data rather than with their preparation.

In addition to making it possible for accounting and financial management to make more timely, detailed, and advanced analyses of the significant areas of business activity, financial and accounting applications have also contributed to more effective decentralization of operations. The wealth of financial information that the computer can make available, its diversity, and its promptness enable each manager to have a better grasp of his operation and to apply greater precision to making changes or controlling situations, at the same time the computer gives top management information for a more precise auditing of the same operational activity. As a consequence, there is greater objectivity in establishing and evaluating operating standards of performance, both from an organizational and from a managerial perspective.

The impact of the computer on the accounting function can best be illustrated by an aerospace company's experience in preparing bids for defense contracts. Because present-day contracts require such detailed cost accounting and performance data, it is virtually impossible for a company to compete in bidding or fulfill a contract effectively without a computerized cost-accounting system.

Marketing. Marketing is another area in which executives have vigorously sought to use the computer, and significant, advanced computer applications have been developed. The most usual applications are routine sales analyses, but some highly sophisticated applications for predicting marketing potential, including marketing simulations, have been developed. In connection with an extensive product-market survey, a division of a food company participating in the study is attempting to predict, with remarkable accuracy, the potential sales of each product on a daily, store-by-store, nationwide basis. Since even the most sophisticated marketing application and its ability to predict are affected by customers' sudden preference changes, the division is now hoping to develop a model incorporating consumer behavioral preference for use in combination with its marketing applications.

The vagaries of consumer preferences are of particular significance in retail marketing, especially because of the effect of seasonal conditions. To contend with this obstacle, the divisions of another company developed a merchandising application wherein buyers could measure customer preferences soon enough to reorder popular items before the demand changed. The company also has market research applications that enable it to decide not only when and where to establish branch stores, but also the size of the store and the appropriate allocation of space to each product department.

A second retailing company uses a retail profit center as a working model for developing merchandising applications, so that through on-site research the computer group can test various operational changes under actual retailing conditions.

One of the most advanced applications is a simulation used in corporate marketing forecasting. The simulation involves a series of marketing models which predict future sales of each of the company's product lines and, under varying conditions, the degree of profitability, capital investment, the need for new plants, warehousing, and the best location for such plants.

Personnel. The personnel function, which would appear to be an ideal area for computer use, is represented by few advanced computer applications. Most applications so far have systematized existing data, and this has offered very little payout as compared to applications in such areas as accounting, marketing, and operations. Also, present applications reflect the fragmentation in personnel specialization. To some extent, applications in other functional areas have obviated the need for computer applications in specific personnel specialities. For example, a computer payroll application may be used effectively in salary or employee benefits administration.

To date, most of the computer applications in personnel have focused on salary administration or some aspect of manpower resources. Numerous companies have developed computerized management manpower inventories designed to identify individuals within the company qualified for advancement or transfer opportunities. Among the study companies, however, only five had developed personnel applications of any significance. These included a salary administration program, a personnel recruitment program, development of a personnel data base, and a program for organization planning.

Research and engineering. In most of the early scientific applications the computer was used as a computational device, and while this represents a substantial area of utilization, the computer is now being used increasingly to substitute for actual laboratory and field experimentation. Not only are a greater number of variables tested in a shorter period of time, but it is also possible to test situations which would be virtually impossible to work out under real conditions, because of the potential danger in the real application.

In any research or engineering-oriented company the computer is a necessity. Even the engineering department of a utility company cannot function without the computer to forecast power load and the need for new equipment and generating stations. An interconnection system among utilities in various states would be a virtual impossibility without the computer.

While the computer has become essential to scientific functions, computer skill has not yet become an integral part of the individual scientist's or engineer's ability to perform his job, but based on the experience of companies to date, there is the implication that this skill will become part of his portfolio in the future. Increasingly, engineers and research personnel will use the computer as a device for solving simple as well as complex problems. In the future, therefore, the capability of scientific personnel, particularly the more recent graduates, may be evaluated in terms of their ability to adapt to computer applications.

Operations. There is little question of the effectiveness of the computer in the operations functions, especially in the manufacturing process and in areas directly related to it. Moreover, computerization in one area tends to stimulate further applications in associated areas. In production scheduling, for example, both the application and the benefits of the computer are increased by the advent of advanced marketing applications; the greater precision and detail of the market forecasts are used most effectively when the production-scheduling system is sufficiently sophisticated to quickly provide the indicated changes in product mix. In many organizations, production scheduling is now a centralized function,

determining the manufacturing operation on a multioperational basis.

The possible impact of the computer application on the production-scheduling function is demonstrated vividly in the refinery operations of one of the study companies. While the refinery operation, per se, is directly under the local refinery management, the computerized production-scheduling application predetermines, in keeping with the market requirements, the optimum selection and distribution of crude oil to the refineries, the refinery's productivity, the product-shipping destination, and the carriers to be used. Through use of the computer, it is possible for a centralized production-scheduling organization to determine the best utilization of the company's overall refinery operations. Changes in production can be scheduled quickly to meet rapidly changing marketing conditions.

The computer application in production scheduling is also of particular importance in the equipment manufacturer's operations. Because of this application, the company is able to coordinate its nationwide interdependent manufacturing operation with its nationwide geographical marketing forecasts and commitments with almost pinpoint accuracy and a minimum of parts inventory.

Corporate planning. The computer has the ability to amass information, simulate, and schedule. This has caused it to have considerable impact upon corporate planning, but it has not fundamentally changed the planning process. The various applications that have evolved in other functional areas, such as in finance and accounting and in marketing, have given top management more diverse and detailed information at a more rapid pace and have provided a sounder basis for corporate planning regarding investment of capital, plant and retailing locations, and new ventures. Notwithstanding the advances that such functional applications make possible, the lack of a corporate-oriented management information system continues to inhibit the evolvement of an innovative management planning process. In a sense, the proposed marketing application of the equipment manufacturer described earlier represents the closest approximation to a corporate management information system.

Both top management and computer personnel are aware of the desirability of, and need for, a corporate management information system. One of the study companies is attempting to determine and develop basic data bases encompassing all of the company's data requirements and to thus develop an information system for corporate management as well as a basis for individual divisional systems.

DETERMINATION OF PRIORITIES OF PROGRAMS AND "BLUE-SKY" DEVELOPMENTS

Although electronic data processing represents a revolution in the management process, computer operations, equipment, and personnel are scarce resources which must be utilized effectively in the development of programs, so that the company as a whole benefits and user organizations are served. The lack of qualified computer personnel affects the extent to which these experts can be assigned to develop specific programs for user organizations and for advanced research or "blue-sky" activities. Yet in every other area of technology related to their operations, companies must undertake a certain amount of research in computer technology to keep from falling behind developments in the computer field and to continue their capability for designing applications that will make significant contributions to company operations.

Many top executives look toward the day when they can feed variables into a company model and observe the range of impacts on various parts of the company. Most of the EDP and management personnel we interviewed expressed the belief that no company can ever realize the full potential of the computer if it does not blue-sky at least some of the time. By this, they meant that some portion of the time of the computer and the data processing personnel should be devoted to model building or simulating, from which, perhaps for long periods of time, no immediate benefit will result. In none of the companies we surveyed did we hear any suggestion that blue-skying was unnecessary or even unprofitable. Rather, both top management and heads of data processing units stressed the activities that were being carried on in their companies in this area and sketched plans for further efforts in the future.

One of the critical determinations an organization must make is the assignment of priorities to program developments and advanced or blue-sky research. Several companies have designated individuals to direct the development of operations models, of long-range planning applications, and, in a few instances, of full-scale corporate models. A number of these men have had difficulty in obtaining either the time needed on the computer or the systems analysts and programmers needed to work on their projects. One corporate long-range planner, frustrated in his efforts to get the company data processing organization to work with him on computerizing some aspects of the planning function, had turned the entire operation over to an outside consultant. He was pleased with the progress of his project but was still irked by having had to go outside the company for action.

Thus, like other potential users of electronic data processing in their companies, blue-skyers encounter the obstacle of limited resources for research. In the assignment of priorities, the long-term and planning aspects of their proposed computer applications tend to net them spots rather far down on the priority list. Somehow, according to some of these men in our study, their positions on the priorities list never seem to improve, since the applications with more immediate return continue to claim the top of the list. Several data processing managers who were aware of the situation lamented the short shrift given planning applications. At the same time, however, they pointed out that much of the information obtained and analyzed through the systems being developed would eventually be helpful in model building and in long-range planning, so that the time devoted to these applications should not be regarded by the planners as totally lost.

Some of the study companies, however, have been somewhat more successful in balancing immediate and long-term applications. In the highly centralized computer operations of three of the study companies, the determination of program priorities and the allocation of resources to blue-sky developments are the responsibility of the central computer departments.

In two of these companies the assignment of priorities to program development is based upon the companywide contribution of the programs. Because of this authority to establish and maintain program priorities, both companies have been able to establish and maintain a planned program of blue-sky developments. In the third company, however, establishing the priorities is somewhat more complex. The determination is the responsibility of the divisions, but the establishment of program priorities is the responsibility of the centralized computer department acting in concert with the divisions. The computer department can determine how much of its resources it can allocate to blue-sky developments, but unlike the other two companies, it must bal-

ance this allocation with the changing demands of the divisional users.

The determination of program priorities and blue-sky developments is more varied and more complex among the companies with a combination of centralized and decentralized computer operations. In one insurance study company the divisions have the authority and staff to develop the programs they desire, but the central computer department has the responsibility and authority to determine the priority in the utilization of computer time. Even though one of the divisions has physical possession of a computer, the allocation of its usage is the responsibility of the central computer group, and this includes the computer's utilization for blue-skying. It must balance the allocation of time to blue-skying with that time allocable to user organizations. The divisional computer departments, however, have the authority to determine what proportion of their resources they wish to allocate to advanced research.

Determination of program priorities and blue-sky operations in a chemical study company is somewhat typical of companies with combined centralized and decentralized computer operations. The divisions that have their own computer hardware and personnel, and that have the responsibility for the development of their own programs, establish priorities for the program development and utilization of the equipment. The corporate computer department, however, has the authority to determine the priority of programs utilizing the central department's computers. In practice, their determination is made in concert with the divisional users. While the individual divisions have the authority to determine the allocation of resources to research developments, this function is primarily the responsibility of the corporate computer department. Here again, the allocation of resources to research developments is conditioned by the need and desire to service the divisions in an adequate manner.

In the highly decentralized computer operations that are characteristic of some of the study companies, the profit-center divisions have the autonomy to determine program priorities and advanced research allocations. However, in one of the companies, in order to prevent duplication of projects, the corporate computer coordinator continually reviews divisional efforts in advanced research. He also keeps abreast of blue-sky developments by computer manufacturers and communicates these to the divisions in order to eliminate efforts which they might be expending on similar developments.

In another decentralized company, centralized computer units within the divisions establish the priority of programs requested by users. For example, the treasurer's division has the authority to determine program priorities for users within that division and, in principle, for its other divisional users. In the latter case, however, it must balance the needs of other divisions against its own need, to fulfill the promise of good service. Each division has the authority to determine resources to be channeled to blue-sky activities. The computer operation in the treasurer's division has a considerable portion of its budget allocated to this, and to prevent duplication in the effort by the other divisions, it uses a quarterly information letter to inform them of its efforts and progress. While its budget allocation for advanced research is considerable, the maintenance of its resources for this function is conditioned by the service demands of its user organizations.

In summary, all of the study companies recognize the need for devoting a certain proportion of their resources to blue-sky research. Where the authority for determination of program priorities and advanced

research is highly centralized, a planned budget can be developed and maintained; where the authority is more diffuse, the result is a more tenuous balance, conditioned by the demands and influences of the user organizations. In some companies that are pursuing aggressive programs aimed at applications to meet immediate needs and yield quick payouts, the short-term application is favored, at the expense, at least temporarily, of blue-sky applications.

Thus a number of companies are in the anomalous position of relying on the capability of the computer to aid in long-range planning and abstract problem solving as, at least in part, its justification, but at the same time actual computer uses for such purposes are largely forestalled by the attention to applications of a short-term nature. This disparity between purpose and accomplishment is an illuminating example of the way in which traditional, precomputer thinking and modes of attacking problems continue to exist in industrial organizations as well as in other institutions. Where this viewpoint prevails, it retards the development of computer applications in areas closely related to the future direction of the company, areas where the potential benefits of such assistance are incalculable.

ACCESS TO THE COMPUTER

In any situation where there is a central computer and some data processing skill in the user divisions, the question of access to the computer facility for programming and machine operation arises. Two opposing schools of thought exist on this point. One is termed the "closed shop" approach while the other is known as the "open shop." As the name implies, the first describes an arrangement whereby the computer room and, usually, programmers are under the direction of a data processing manager through whom time on the equipment and programmer time must be obtained. The other term covers a much more laissez-faire situation, where users have almost unlimited access to the computer room and the programmers, with the role of the data processing manager becoming almost that of a mere schedule keeper.

Although there was some degree of variation in the ease of computer room accessibility among the companies we studied, none approached the epitome of the open shop. Employees of user divisions in a few of the companies work closely with the data processing group, spending a great deal of time in the computer room. But this reflects the capability of individuals in the user divisions rather than an organizational avenue to the computer room. Moreover, work done by user personnel in the computer area is conducted in conjunction with, not independent of, the computer personnel. Without exception, the executives who expressed opinions on the subject were firmly opposed to the unlimited entree to the computer facility inherent in the open-shop concept.

5. Conflict Arising from Location and Control of the Computer Complex

SOME CONFLICT OVER THE LO-cation and control of the computer and the purposes for which it should be used is inevitable. And although a measure of conflict may keep an organization on its toes, too much of it may impede realization of the full benefits of computer application. The real issue is the manner in which conflict is resolved. EDP managers and other members of top management are moving in a number of ways to deal early with organizational dislocations stemming from the decision to computerize and to minimize the tensions that sometimes build up when computer uses are expanded.

Conflict may stem from a number of sources. One is the unplanned, haphazard way in which the computer typically has been introduced. Others are: differing views as to the costs and benefits of proposed applications and the designation of applications that are to have priority; differing standards among decentralized units; and differing evaluations of the need for additional hardware and the kind needed.

Organizational Conflict

During the initial upsurge in a company's demand for computer capability, operating and functional divisions within the same company often approached computer vendors independently, without attempting to determine what action was being contemplated or was under way elsewhere in the organization. They succeeded in obtaining computers for their own proposed applications, since vendors usually did not try to influence them as to where an installation should or should not be located (except by their implicit belief that each possible location should have its own computer).

LACK OF PLANNING FOR EDP

Historically, the degree to which computer facilities were established on an uncoordinated, independent-need basis was related to the amount of autonomy that an individual organizational unit had. During the 1950's and early 1960's industry in general was moving toward decentralized operations, establishing profit centers and delegating greater decision-making responsibility to autonomous functional units at all levels. In many organizations the major limitations to operating autonomously were financial—the need to function within an approved budget and obtain specific authorization for capital expenditures. Even in the financial area the trend toward greater delegation of decision-making responsibility was apparent, as authority for large capital expenditures was increasingly granted without the necessity of seeking corporate approval. Moreover, the opportunity to lease computers rather than invest in outright purchase increased the number of organizational units that could install them within the limits of their financial authorizations. Thus the original decision as to where within an organization the computer should be located was a result of the unit's needs and the extent of its autonomy, along with the tacit approval that came from management's unawareness of the computer's potential and broad ramifications. These circumstances explain the diversity of conditions under which the computer was introduced and its disparate locations within the study companies.

As a result of this uncoordinated approach, a number of computer centers and organizations were created in operating and functional divisions. These organizations quickly acquired all of the political overtones and organizational trappings of power and vested self-interest. In other words, separate centers became the status quo, and subsequent efforts to consolidate hardware and determine where future computer applications should logically be located encountered the resistance usually accorded attempts to rock the establishment. Companies with the need and desire to centralize—either totally or partially—the EDP activities of these fiefs thus had to adopt various strategies to attain their end.

1. *Placing the function at a high executive level* was an approach that one insurance company took to this problem. The impetus for acquiring a computer had come from the group-insurance division, one of three autonomous operating divisions. Its business activity had expanded very rapidly, and it was faced with a steadily mounting volume of administrative records to process. Was the solution to acquire additional clerical personnel and tabulating equipment? A

review of the projected workload indicated not only that it would be virtually impossible to recruit enough clerical personnel, but that available office space would not accommodate the number of employees that would be needed. This brought up the question of whether the division should acquire a computer. A subsequent feasibility study signaled divisional top management to go ahead. While awaiting computer delivery, however, the division engaged an outside service bureau to undertake a thorough systems analysis, and the acquisition was further postponed until internal systems and programs had been developed. Finally, the division acquired the initial hardware plus a second computer a few years later, and it operated the installation autonomously for several years. Meanwhile, the other two operating divisions also initiated computer feasibility studies, thereby alerting corporate management to both the computer's potential and the implications of having separate organizational units "in business" with their own independent computer complexes. Management then decided that a central operation would best serve overall company needs but initially located the operation in the controller's division and allowed the group division to maintain its own installation with as much autonomy as before. The centralized computer operation in the controller's division did not work out well. This was because (1) it lacked the necessary computer and systems personnel to carry out its objectives and responsibilities effectively, and (2) as merely one of many functions in the controller's division, it did not have sufficient organizational autonomy. Consequently, the centralized computer operation, along with systems planning and corporate planning and research, was transferred into a separate division, headed by a vice president who was well versed in both the operations and EDP.

Under this stronger guidance, the central

computer services began to operate more effectively. But the life and casualty divisions, while using the central computer services, were able to retain their programmers and systems personnel. And, although in principle, computer hardware was the responsibility of the central computer service department, the group division, for all practical purposes, was able to maintain its own complete computer complex. It was only through the direct involvement of a knowledgeable vice president that the company was able to achieve its desired end—an increasingly centralized approach to computer activities in the company and the retention of a degree of autonomy in each of the three divisions.

2. *Forming a central computer capability side by side with the divisional operations and asking the divisions to participate in task-force projects* was a method used by a retailing firm to overcome divisions' resistance to centralizing EDP. In this firm the computer was first used in 1957 at one of the profit centers to develop an accounts-receivable system. The system was not as effective as expected, and its cost discouraged the corporate headquarters and the other profit centers from undertaking any further computer activity for several years. In 1961, however, when several profit centers established computer operations, management saw the opportunity to evaluate the effectiveness of different approaches and to attain an overall benefit for the corporation. As a result, a central corporate data processing complex was established to develop systems and programs that would be beneficial to all profit centers.

The corporate approach to preserving the autonomy of the profit centers was to invite several of them to participate in experimental systems development, initially in the area of inventory control, and then offer successful systems to other profit centers. The headquarters data processing group then de-

veloped another experimental system for merchandising. A profit-center divisional merchandising information group headed this system development. Again, use of the system was left to the individual division's discretion. Under this voluntary approach the divisions have concentrated essentially on developing systems that meet their own operating requirements, while the headquarters data processing center has worked on (1) systems that are valuable and applicable to all divisions but that divisions may decline to accept, and (2) management information systems for corporate management planning.

In effect, then, what has been attempted here is to provide the needed capability at the corporate level, use this capability to obtain important companywide information, and at the same time encourage the divisions to make use of the headquarters facility. In the process, this has provided broader coverage for the corporate information system by making available to divisions the corporate group's knowledge, skill, and hardware.

Companies using this technique of centralizing rely on the force of example to obtain divisional consensus. It is believed that as the divisions observe the competence and ability of the corporate group and the applications it has devised for other divisions, they, in turn, will use the corporate facilities as a kind of service bureau. Such an approach avoids direct confrontation between the central computer group and those in the divisions, which would retard computerization in some companies. Necessarily, achieving centralization by this approach is a slow process.

CENTRALIZED EDP AS A THREAT TO DIVISIONAL AUTONOMY

The organizational impact, real or imagined, of centralizing or decentralizing computer operations has perhaps given rise to the greatest conflict over how the computer should be utilized. The very existence of the computer, and its enormous capacity to handle, process, and disseminate information, is regarded by many division managers as a threat to their autonomy, and as a result, the location of the computer complex within the organization is of considerable moment to them. Indeed, the prospect of conflict between traditional management-organization relationships in a highly decentralized and divisionalized company with the policies and operations of a centralized computer organization may lead a company to forgo, at least temporarily, some of the advantages of a consolidated EDP approach and to permit the divisions to continue to operate their own computer activities autonomously.

The prospect of conflict arises because of confusion over what "centralization" and "decentralization" of the computer really mean and what their potential implications are. To most management people a decentralized organization is equated with having greater autonomy and decision-making authority at lower levels, while centralization means more autonomy and decision-making power resting within, or directed upward, toward the corporate level. In a number of the study companies, almost invariably the centralization-decentralization issue involving the computer function was treated as if it were identical to centralization or decentralization of the corporate organizational structure and style of management. This concept of the centralization-decentralization issue inhibited achievement of centralized EDP operations by these companies, even when they considered centralization desirable. In other companies the philosophical commitment to decentralization and concomitant autonomy and decision-making power is so pervasive that decentralized EDP operations are accepted and

supported without question. Yet others whose commitment to decentralized operations is just as strong, in practice as well as in principle, are gradually centralizing EDP on a planned basis in the belief that not only will this *not* diminish the autonomy and decision-making power of decentralized divisions, but it will enhance the effectiveness of the divisions as well as of the whole company.

Examples of different ways of dealing with this situation occurred in two chemical companies in the study. These companies, doing business in the same industry and strongly dedicated to the decentralized, divisionalized concept, chose very different places for computer operations in their organizations.

1. In one chemical company the computer was initially introduced by the product divisions to meet their own needs, primarily for accounting, sales analysis, and research. During the 1950's, corporate management conducted a three-year study to determine the feasibility of a headquarters computer complex. This brought about the decision to establish the computer operation as an independent division, to develop systems that were applicable companywide, and to provide a service bureau for divisions that had no computers. Development of systems that crossed divisional lines required the voluntary participation of the divisions, since they were still free to develop their own independently. In cases where only some of them participated in systems development, the computer complex directed its effort toward offering the new system to the nonparticipating divisions.

The operations of the corporate computer complex continued to advance, but management felt that overall computer activities were insufficiently planned and coordinated. At about this time the controller's function had been transferred from the treasurer's division and established as a separate division. This enlarged function was responsible for the more significant aspects of corporate long-range planning. Besides this, the corporate controller had considerable experience in both product division operations and treasury functions. He took a broad corporate view of company activities. As a result, the corporate computer complex was transferred to the controller's division. Another factor contributing to this decision was that each division had a controller's office, and those divisions with computer operations had placed responsibility for it within the controller's section.

Total company EDP efforts are now highly coordinated at the corporate level through the corporate controller. Although each division has autonomy for its own computer and its operations, it must review and seek approval for any additional hardware acquisition. In addition, it must review with corporate EDP the feasibility, cost, and contribution to the divisional organization of any proposal for developing a major system. At the same time the review will point out any potential duplication of planned companywide systems development. The corporate group also develops standards, which are correlated throughout the company. The coordinative function is performed by corporate account executive liaisons. Each such executive must know the scope and future plans of both corporate and divisional computer activities, in addition to developments taking place within the division he represents. While conflicts still arise over the costs and benefits of proposed programs and the need for hardware, this approach minimizes the number and intensity of potential clashes between corporate and divisional computer users, since it tends to resolve potential conflicts at an early stage rather than allowing them to break out at the point when systems are being implemented.

2. In the other chemical company the engineering division made the initial proposal to acquire a computer for technical and scientific purposes. This sparked an accounting division bid for a computer to process accounting and business data. As a result, top management decided to acquire a single machine for both the engineering and treasurer's divisions, while a study committee determined future needs. At the end of the two-year study, the engineering division was given responsibility for the existing computer and the treasurer's division acquired another one, each retaining complete autonomy for its operations. The treasurer's division organized its computer operation as a business systems section within the controller's department and headed it with a director at a level comparable to assistant controller.

As interest spread throughout the company, computer operations were established at divisional, plant, and research-laboratory organizational levels, each operating independently of any central coordination and control. Each division allocated EDP responsibility to an analysis and business section in its control function, a counterpart of the business systems section in the controller's department. Despite the fact that the controller's department reports functionally to the corporate controller's department, its operations are autonomous, reporting directly to the division general manager. All divisions must conform to prescribed accounting and control procedures and report data in a standard format, but divisions are free to process the data as they choose, using tabulating equipment, computer, or outside service bureaus. Some divisions and plants chose to use the facilities of the accounting or the engineering divisions, but this decision was purely discretionary. Apparently, no conflict has arisen over computer uses, since each major organizational unit is able to establish and operate its own installation at will and to acquire hardware and systems through the normal channels of authority for capital expenditures.

The principle of autonomous organizational responsibility for the computer remains essentially unchallenged today. Yet in practice the pattern is changing as the impact of the third-generation computers is felt and as the corporate business system section perceives the economies and efficiencies that can be achieved by more centralized EDP. Thus, while continuing to accept the divisions' and plants' autonomy, the corporate controller's departmental computer group, by demonstrating its ability to provide cost savings and better service, has attempted to convince these plants and divisions to transfer their data processing operations to the controller's department.

Though this approach has been successful, it has also presented an area of conflict. Since the corporate business system section acts as a service bureau for the user divisions, the divisions can decide what systems or programs should be developed; and while the corporate group may attempt to convince a "customer" that a particular program has limited value or that another one would be more effective, it is the customer who is willing to pick up the tab who has the ultimate authority. Therefore, to maintain good relations and keep the customer, the corporate group must comply with the division's request.

Examining the study company organizations, however, reveals different concepts of what the impact of centralizing EDP operations will be. The two chemical companies, for example, are quite similar in organization structure and without question are equally committed to decentralization in the form of autonomous profit-center divisions. But one company has followed this operational concept through permissive decentralization of computer responsibility and use, while the other has taken the opposite route. The philosophy of the first company, somewhat oversimplified, is that if a manager of an organizational unit is to be accountable for the unit's operating results, he must have authority for all the functions that contribute to achieving results. In line with this charter, he should not only have the discretion to use or not to use the service functions, but he should also have the power to employ similar outside services if he believes conditions warrant it. Thus each autonomous unit may determine its own means of processing data. The wisdom of the choice will be reflected in the results.

The second chemical company, also committed to decentralization and autonomous profit centers, has established a centralized EDP unit (at corporate headquarters) with relatively strong coordination and control of divisional EDP operations. Corporate management knows that central coordination and control increase the likelihood of disagreement between the corporate and divisional EDP operations, but it does not believe this coordination is a threat to organizational decentralization and autonomy. On the other hand, management is convinced that central control contributes to the divisions' effectiveness and efficiency. However, the corporate EDP department exercises its coordinative and control function carefully, trying to enhance the stature and autonomy of divisional EDP operations and minimize corporate-divisional conflicts. This is because the department is aware of the divisions' fear that a corporate department that coordinates and controls companywide EDP operations may impinge somewhat upon divisional autonomy and, more important, that this may portend greater centralization of overall divisional activities. Corporate EDP uses a divisional account executive to help divisions develop economical and beneficial programs and forestall serious potential disagreements by resolving them as early as possible. While the fact that the corporate controller must approve a division's request to acquire computer hardware seemingly reduces divisional authority, favorable EDP department review enhances a division's chances of receiving the approval of the controller or of higher management. Overall, greater centralized coordination and control are seen as a means of realizing and supporting organizational decentralization and autonomy.

The approaches of two other companies in retailing illustrate still other variations on the two different attitudes toward centralizing EDP operations. Both these corporate managements also are committed to organizational decentralization and autonomy. Yet one has limited the scope of the EDP centralization because it does not wish to infringe upon the organizational autonomy of its divisional profit centers, while the other has maximized EDP centralization without considering this a threat to profit-center autonomy or to the concept of organizational decentralization.

In the first retailing company, central computer activities have been limited primarily to corporate-level information programs for management research and planning. While management wants to develop programs that have companywide application, concern for protecting divisional autonomy has caused it to approach this objective by establishing a voluntary program task force composed of divisional profit-center representatives. The corporate EDP group contributes systems knowledge and guidance. Task-force leadership is rotated, being placed for each program with the person from the divisions who is considered most knowledgeable in the program's subject area. The corporate group may initiate companywide development programs, but actual program development and implementation depend on the willingness of the divisional profit centers to participate. The divisions have not been enthusiastic about participating in such developments. Essen-

tially, the corporate EDP group must sell them on the potential value of programs. In short, divisional profit centers use their EDP operations to develop programs to meet their own specific needs, and they call on the corporate group for advice or consultation only as they need it. Management would prefer the corporate computer group to have greater control over divisional computer groups, but it finds it difficult to achieve this goal without seeming to violate divisional autonomy.

The second retailing company has completely centralized, companywide EDP operations as a matter of corporate policy. The corporate EDP department fully coordinates and controls the acquisition of equipment and the selection and development of programs, standards, and operating procedures. Even the personnel who are to represent the corporate functional areas as liaison to the corporate EDP operations must be approved by the corporate group. Yet this comprehensive centralization does not abridge the divisional profit centers' autonomy or interfere with their operations. In fact, the corporate EDP group's research simulation of operating conditions contributes to the profit centers' operating effectiveness. Beyond that, using the corporate EDP function as a planned rotational and training phase for functional liaison personnel also contributes to the future effectiveness of the operating profit centers. The basic requirement for successfully establishing a centralized EDP function, while maintaining the concept and practice of organizational decentralization and autonomy, is understanding among both corporate and divisional managers of the relationship between organizational decentralization and centralized EDP.

LOCATION OF EDP IN A FUNCTIONAL AREA

The location of the computer complex in a functional area, such as accounting or engineering, also arouses conflict in some situations. Managers of other functional areas may feel that the manager with the computer complex will apply its capability to his own operations at the expense of the others—and indeed, this may actually happen. One of the sharpest conflicts of this kind arose in one of the study companies when the manager of engineering found the computer complex located in the financial and accounting division, practically inaccessible to him. In another company, where the computer complex related to business systems had been located in the accounting function, corporate management decided that a more comprehensive information system was required, and that it could be developed most effectively under the direction of a vice president who reported directly to the president. This decision raised the question of whether EDP would continue to be applied to the rather substantial accounting system. Considerable EDP knowledge and experience, as well as a separate computer facility, existed in the accounting function. The accounting executive and his staff were reluctant to surrender this capability, which they regarded as essential to their operations. The problem and the potential conflict were resolved by permitting the accounting function to retain both its computer facility and its EDP personnel and by establishing a separate computer facility and EDP corps for broader information systems development. Probably, however, the accounting EDP operation will eventually be absorbed into the separate data processing/information systems function. In the meantime the either-or choice has been avoided, and conflict that might have arisen from such a choice has been headed off. Time is expected to ease tension and permit the merger of the two operations with a minimum of internal disruption.

Although the location of the EDP-based information systems activity in a particular function may lead to organizational strain, so may the creation of a separate data processing and information systems function. As we have seen in the preceding illustration, management of the company foresaw the potential trouble and acted to avoid it. In another highly divisionalized company, the data processing operation was removed from the accounting and control function and made into a separate department reporting directly to top management. While the accounting and control organization continues to have a strong part in determin-computer applications for informational purposes, a potential trouble spot would exist if more of the informational systems development function were transferred to the data processing vice president. Accounting and control personnel in this company maintain that the control function is inherent to any management information system, and that if the controller is to continue to have responsibility for the company's control function, he must play a pivotal role in determining the feasibility of EDP applications for the information system. Sharing responsibility for the development of an effective companywide computer-based information system has apparently worked for the year or so that this policy has been in existence. But the fact that the controller has traditional responsibility—sole responsibility—for the control function, which is one of the aspects of the information system, while the data processing manager has no such responsibility for an end use of the information system, contains the seeds of potential difficulty.

Procedural Conflicts

While managers who are accustomed to operating in a decentralized environment may oppose the *concept* of centralization in any form, specific applications of the procedures necessary to create consolidated EDP may also arouse considerable disagreement and resistance. The procedural questions around which debate may center include: (1) Where should the authority to approve acquisition of computer equipment be vested? (2) Should it be rented or purchased? (3) Who should be responsible for operating the equipment? And perhaps the knottiest question of all (4) How should the needs and order of priority of proposed computer applications be assessed and allocated among a number of computer users?

When a company decides to centralize all or most of its computer operations, conflicts are stirred up over these questions if EDP users are accustomed to making such decisions themselves. Here is how some of the study companies resolved such questions on the road to attaining consolidated status for EDP.

CONFLICTS OVER PURCHASE OF EQUIPMENT

In one insurance company where all the computer activities and operations are centralized in headquarters offices, the assistant vice president in charge of central data processing recommends the purchase of needed equipment to his superior, and this recommendation is subjected to approval by top management. Similarly, in another study company where computer equipment and operations are geographically dispersed, the corporate central data processing department has full authority to determine the need for, and purchase of, EDP equipment for the company. Even regional requests for peripheral equipment purchases are subject to complete central review and approval.

Although, in a third study company, the accounting department operates its own computer complex for processing accounting and financial data, this essentially is because all corporate data processing is being consolidated into a central data processing division, and eventually accounting data processing operations will be included within it. Meanwhile, accounting needs and purchases of equipment are determined by top management in consultation with the vice president in charge of the central data processing department.

In all these cases, the potential conflict over the purchase of computer equipment is resolved by top management's establishing definitive organizational authority for the purchases.

Conflict over who should have authority for determining equipment needs and purchases is more marked in companies that are moving toward EDP centralization but have not yet arrived at that point. In these companies, management usually has as an objective the more effective utilization of companywide EDP activities. The objective can be realized in part by corporate control of computer equipment purchases. The division's objective is usually to develop programs it considers necessary for its operation, and this means acquiring equipment needed to operate its own computer installations. While following normal corporate channels of control for equipment purchases may be acceptable to divisional management, vesting authority for determining the need for, and the purchase of, equipment in a central EDP group implies, to some divisional managers, a threat to their operational autonomy. In the view of a divisional general manager, if he is to have complete accountability for his operating results he should be free to purchase any equipment he considers necessary to achieve those results. (Or as he says, "Judge me on the results, not on what it takes to get them.")

The problem of the centralized computer department is to achieve the corporate objective—effective utilization of company-wide EDP activities—while simultaneously helping divisions to satisfy their EDP needs without interfering with their operational autonomy. This problem is made more acute by the potential conflict between the immediate, short-range outlook of the divisions toward their equipment needs and the broad, long-range view of the central computer group. For example, a number of divisions may feel that their immediate or near-term data processing requirements or efficiency would be best served by purchasing new computers or supplementary equipment, the costs of which they are quite willing to accept. The centralized computer group may agree with each individual division's estimate of the near-term value that will accrue to the division, but it may also be aware of the possibility that more advanced or sophisticated computers may serve the needs of all divisions at a lower overall cost. The corporate computer group is also aware of the natural desire of the divisional computer groups to acquire the most advanced computer on the market and thus to unconsciously evaluate their needs and the suitability and real utilization of their present computers less critically. The centralized computer unit must evaluate the alternatives objectively if it is to achieve corporate goals and yet assure the divisions that their needs will be satisfied.

Here are some instances in which companies have encountered these internal conflicts in various forms and are moving to reduce or remove them.

In one study company the possibility of disagreement over who should determine whether hardware is needed, and who should have authority to purchase it, is slight, because there is no central computer complex as yet, and there probably will not be for some time. As a result, each division's equipment purchase requests are evaluated primarily in relation to the division's spe-

cific needs. The potential for conflict does exist, however, in differing corporate and divisional evaluations of the division's effectiveness in programming and its utilization of the computer installation. The corporate view is to strive to tighten up programming and improve applications to get the most effective use of the present computer and avoid the premature need for purchasing additional equipment. The approach to this area of conflict is to establish objective performance standards that will guide the divisions toward greater effectiveness and also serve to measure the divisions' performance. The corporate office also offers technical guidance and supports the divisions' efforts to attain greater effectiveness.

Disagreement can also arise over the selection of equipment. The corporate objective is to achieve a compatible companywide configuration, anticipating the future when possibly regional or corporate centralization will take place. In striving to meet its objective and avoid clashes over divisional equipment preferences, the corporate computer coordinator must understand the particular requirements of each division and the probable timing of future requirements and then determine the equipment that is both compatible with that of other divisions and applicable to the specific division's needs. The corporate coordinator's ability to demonstrate the potential advantages of the desired equipment and the opportunities that arise from having compatible equipment with which divisions can interchange programs and applications eliminates much potential conflict. Further, the lengthy period allowed for developing compatible hardware reduces the likelihood that disagreements will take place.

The approach taken toward removing the possibility of conflicts in another company reflects its desire to avoid infringing upon divisional operating autonomy. In a sense the conflict regarding the authority for equipment purchase takes place at the corporate management level. Although the corporate data processing group believes corporate control of equipment purchase would be the most efficient, corporate management may not be willing to impose this condition upon the divisions. To effect "control" over divisional equipment purchases, the corporate EDP group makes it a practice to continually consult divisions about their EDP needs, program development, staffing, and the appropriateness of equipment to fulfill their needs. The corporate EDP group recognizes the authority of the divisions but attempts to influence them by performing as a consulting service bureau, offering expert advice and guidance. The corporate group hopes that good relations between the two organizations will resolve conflict and stimulate divisional acceptance of, and reliance upon, corporate counseling. Thus, divisional equipment purchase decisions result from corporate-divisional discussions, in which corporate expertise has its influence.

Among study companies that do not have centralized corporate EDP, authority for determining the need for, and purchase of, computer equipment rests primarily with divisions but is subject to advisory committee review. In the decentralized EDP organizational setting in one company, the divisions have authority for equipment purchase—that is, the divisional EDP operation's request for equipment purchase or lease requires the division manager's approval. All computer requisitions are reviewed by an advisory committee composed of the largest divisional computer users in the company, but the committee's role is purely advisory, not controlling. The corporate treasurer is officially informed of purchase or lease of computers anywhere in the company.

Another study company also has an advisory committee that studies and evaluates the companywide need for EDP and the most appropriate method of acquiring and utilizing the equipment. While the study is being carried on, no new large-scale equipment can be purchased. Peripheral equipment for the accounting or engineering department is acquired as needed and approved by the corporate management committee.

CONFLICTS OVER NEED, FEASIBILITY, AND PRIORITIES OF PROGRAMS

Perhaps the greatest continuing source of conflict, regardless of whether computer activity is centralized or located within the divisions, stems from determining the feasibility of proposed applications and assigning time and equipment priorities for those that are approved. This problem confronts divisional and corporate EDP organizations alike but becomes more serious when a central facility strives to serve the needs of a wide variety of user organizations. Like any manager of a limited resource who is serving a number of users, the manager of a centralized EDP operation must ration money, personnel, time, and equipment to meet demands that exceed his supply.

The centralization of EDP within the corporate organizational structure, evident in at least five study companies, and emerging in the EDP operations of a sixth company, means that the corporate EDP group must be able to satisfy the divisional needs at least as effectively as they could be satisfied on a decentralized basis.

In one company the right to determine need, feasibility, and priorities has been fully vested, through top management policy and mandate, in the centralized data processing department. A program proposal is weighed for its potential contribution to the company as a whole; the same criterion is used for establishing priorities, except that the schedule may be modified if a particular functional customer has a critical need. In practice, the liaison personnel represent the needs of their functional organizations—merchandising, credit, accounting —and provide the functional knowledge on the potential program to enable the EDP group to evaluate the program's feasibility and desirability and its priority status in relation to other programs that may be equally feasible and desirable. Although the EDP operation is supported by a sizable budget, it obviously is confronted with more proposed applications than it can undertake at any particular time, so that priorities must be established. The EDP department painstakingly explains the reasons for low priorities or for nonacceptability of an idea. Though customers have the right to seek from top management a change in the EDP decision, they rarely do this, since top management has essentially delegated its authority in this area to the experts in the central data processing department, and results to date, in top management's view, have justified this delegation. (The central data processing department makes periodic presentations to top management to keep members informed on what is going on.)

The authority vested in the central data processing department also enables it to establish research and development computer needs and priorities. Unlike the situation in many companies, the department does not have to divert blue-sky research manpower and money to provide functional service in order to retain customers.

The basic corporate policy and authority delegation that support EDP in this case are also characteristic of another study company's centralized component. The central EDP department determines the feasibility of programs and assigns priority on the basis of obtaining the greatest benefit to the company as a whole. The chances of these responsibilities being authoritatively and objectively implemented are enhanced by the fact that the EDP manager is a vice president who reports directly to the president, and further, that this vice president has broad companywide managerial experience in diverse functions. His long association with top management makes him a particularly effective communicator of the benefits that the company will achieve through a particular application, and particularly well qualified to determine priorities fairly.

Again here, as in the other company, central EDP uses liaison personnel from the user functions to establish needs, to provide the information necessary to determine the possibilities of a particular program, and in a large part, to provide the input information for developing it. Careful, detailed, long-range planning of organizational structure and functioning, training and development needs, and project-scheduling requirements has enabled central EDP to establish priorities for a comprehensive schedule of project applications while maintaining its own research and development plan.

Another study company represents a somewhat different centralized data processing situation. As part of its campaign to get the divisions to use the computer more fully, the corporation promised them that they would receive outstanding service and benefits. To generate "business," they were allowed great latitude in determining their needs. Whereas feasibility was previously determined by the technical capability of a program being developed, now a program was acceptable to the central data processing group if a division were willing to pay for it. Priorities were of little consequence. Today, however, the division and the corporate EDP organization share responsibility for determining need. The EDP group investigates corporate needs, endorses those programs that meet these needs, and solicits financial support from the divisions for program development. The individual needs of each division are determined by the division and central EDP together. Since EDP personnel are, by this time, quite familiar with division operations, they may suggest areas in which computer application might be beneficial to them. While the divisions still have the authority to insist on programs if they are willing to pay for them, the central EDP group exerts greater influence and control over decisions, with respect to the cost and value of a program. Disagreement over whether to undertake a program has been slight because (1) the divisions have become more knowledgeable about desirable applications, and (2) the EDP group is anxious to conserve its resources for really beneficial programs.

Priorities are more of a problem now that the benefits of the computer are known to all divisions. The central EDP group attempts to evaluate the demands objectively and balance divisions' needs. While the divisions may exert pressure to move up favorite programs on the time schedule, they are also realistically aware of competing pressures and tend to accept, if reluctantly at times, the decision of the EDP group. The division liaison personnel, with a greater understanding of the EDP operations than their associates in the division, are also able to moderate divisional demands for priority. In addition, managers generally agree that the EDP group reaches its decision on priority by giving weight to the applications that will contribute the most to the overall effectiveness of the company.

Still, in attempting to provide the divisions with the best possible service, corporate EDP faces an internal problem, inasmuch as it must meet the division's deadline at the expense of some long-range, blue-sky research. The corporate group tries to adhere to its research schedule, realizing the future value of research, but when the need is urgent, it will divert some of its research resources to the service of the divisions.

One insurance company has an unusual method of determining program need, feasibility, and priority. The primary decision that a program is necessary rests with the functional organizational units. The central EDP group can also make studies to determine whether a proposed application will be beneficial to the organizational units, but it has no authority to implement the studies. Further, the EDP unit can only encourage the divisions and departments to use its services. To reduce the area of potential conflict, the organization and procedures department, which reports to the president, has—as part of its responsibility for overall cost reduction through improved methods and procedures—the task of identifying cost-reduction areas appropriate for computer application. Through the influence of the office of the president, such areas become prime targets for computer group study and programs. Feasibility is determined by the EDP department primarily on the basis of cost savings. If a program is possible and the customer wants it and is willing to absorb the cost, the computer group will develop it. The EDP group also has the authority for determining priorities. To some extent, priorities have not really been a problem, since the department has been able to staff its organization to carry out scheduled projects. Where users have demanded priority, the EDP group has been able to adjust its schedule to realize greater cost savings. This approach has won relatively good acceptance. However, increasing use of the computer facilities for applications other than those concerned with cost savings will make it more difficult to establish the precedence of various projects in the future.

In another insurance company, EDP coordination and control are centralized, but a profit-center division has its own computer. It is the profit center's responsibility, in fact, to determine both need and initial feasibility, although the central data processing service reviews these decisions. The profit-center division, like the other divisions, controls its own priorities. The central data processing section primarily decides what the service division needs, whether such potential applications are feasible, and in what order they will be scheduled and applied.

As the experiences of these study companies show, either the user organizations retain the final say on the feasibility of applications and their priority or the management of the company vests this authority with a central EDP manager. In actual practice, as the company experiences bear out, the most effective means of diminishing conflict in these areas has been to involve the user organizations in the process of determining feasibility and to have the users themselves determine their own priorities. This is an imperfect device, but it has offered the most lasting and effective means of reducing friction. Most of the companies studied provide, either formally or informally, a means of appeal to higher authority to resolve the exceptional situation where severe conflict does arise. A few managements have attempted to reduce the number of such appeals by setting forth broad guidelines for the EDP manager and the heads of user organizations to aid them in resolving differences among themselves. But it is unrealistic to expect that such guidelines will totally eliminate differences of opinion that cannot

be accommodated, and in such cases, top management renders the final judgment.

Summary

As we observed earlier in this chapter, conflict within an organization is inevitable, and to a degree, healthy. If one considers the vast potential of the computer and what its uses can mean to the individual manager and his operation, it is little wonder that its location in the organization and the authority to control its use have engendered debate. Indeed, it is surprising that these questions have not created more debate. We have tried to show how some of the companies in this study are dealing with this problem. Clearly, there is no one way that will apply to all companies. But despite the lack of a universal conflict-solvent, a general conclusion can be drawn. The passage of time and the greater sophistication arising out of long experience in expanding computer applications appear to be the most effective means of overcoming internal rivalries. The companies that have applied the computer intensively, extensively, and with imagination to the challenge of information systems, and that have been successful in this, appear to be the least troubled by internal rivalries. Further, it appears that the successful use of EDP has reduced its conflict potential instead of magnifying it.

Appendix I. Case Histories of Computer

Operations in Study Companies

Case 1:
International Chemical and Drug Manufacturer

Domestically, the company is organized along functional lines, with autonomous nationwide product divisions. Functional units within each of the divisions reflect those found at the corporate level.

The computer complex is centered at corporate headquarters; supplementary installations of varying degrees of sophistication are found at eight locations across the United States and at four locations overseas. The corporate installation consists of IBM 7070, 1401, and 360 equipment, and the RCA Spectra 70/15. At the field locations the equipment is quite varied, being determined by specific local needs. An increasing number of company locations without computer installations of their own, but with EDP needs, are being connected to the corporate installation by telecommunication devices.

At the corporate level, responsibility for data processing is assigned to the corporate controller. Within the divisions, data processing activities are directed by the division controllers, who report on both line and functional matters to the corporate controller and administratively to their respective division general managers.

Eight years ago the controller's division was separated from the treasurer's function because of the controller's growing involvement in the planning process. This change proved to be highly significant for the evolution of the computer complex, for in 1962 responsibility for computer operations was relocated in the newly created controller's division. Until this time it had reported to top management. The controller's function was considered the logical place for the activity because of its emphasis on planning; moreover, in several of the divisions where computers were being utilized, the responsibility for computer operations had been assigned to the division controller.

Today, the corporate controller, who is a broad-gauged individual with considerable experience in nonaccounting phases of company operations, has direct responsibility for the areas traditionally associated with his function, as well as for most of the significant management planning functions, including operations analysis and administrative studies, economic analysis, and computer application analysis.

The computer-related aspects of the controller's function are largely under the director of data processing, who reports to an assistant controller. The data processing group includes some 150 people, some of whom have EDP backgrounds, while others have had specific experience in operational and functional areas of the company.

As shown in Exhibit A, the data processing group is organized into several subgroups. Three of these relate to the operation of a computer installation, including machine operations, programming, and the purchase and rental of equipment. Other subgroups are concerned with divisional operations and needs. One unit is concerned, for example, with finance, marketing, and administrative applications, while another directs its attention primarily to applications in the research, engineering, and manufacturing areas. All major data processing actions proposed by the divisions must be submitted to the corporate controller for approval. In operation, this means that he approves all equipment acquisitions above a certain amount.

The data processing group participates both in the feasibility studies for proposed applications in the divisions and in the decisions to adopt or abandon proposed projects. It provides the necessary data on the cost of computerizing proposed programs, advises on the availability of EDP staff and

EXHIBIT A. *Structure of Central Data Processing Unit*

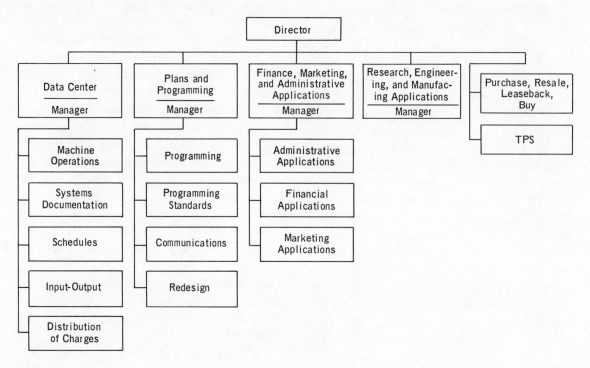

computer time for implementing these programs, and assists in deciding whether the application under consideration is best suited to electronic equipment or manual devices. The user divisions are charged for development and operations work; thus they take a direct interest in the ultimate feasibility of any proposed application. This corporate–divisional relationship has been a key element in the development of the programs in effect in user divisions.

The corporate data processing staff is acutely aware of the autonomy of the divisions and of the concern among some divisional executives that computer technology may erode their authority. Consequently, in its approach, the corporate staff emphasizes guiding and counseling. Except for major applications, the decision on whether to proceed with a program usually rests with the user division if there is lack of agreement between corporate and user staffs.

Such disagreements have arisen only rarely, however.

Overall, the course toward increased divisional use of computerized systems is a gradual one, with the corporate staff helping the divisions strike a balance between over- or underutilization of EDP.

At the corporate level the computer was used initially for sales analysis, and this application is still an important one. This area was selected for the first corporate computer project because it offered greater possibilities for realizing a money saving than the other possible choice, accounting. Moreover, manufacturing locations had adequate accounting systems utilizing both EDP and manual equipment. Currently, the data processing group is broadening computer applications on a companywide basis. Among the applications being developed are a sophisticated accounts-receivable program and an order-billing operation.

EXHIBIT B. *Corporate Location of Computer Operations*

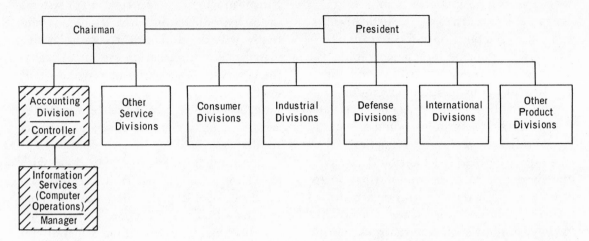

Case 2:
International Electrical and Electronic Equipment Manufacturer

The overall organizational structure of this large international company is characterized by centralized service divisions and highly autonomous, decentralized, profit-center product groups and divisions. The profit centers report to the president and chief executive officer; the service divisions, to the chairman of the board. The company is noted for advanced research in support of its product development and for long-range planning of its business endeavors.

Experience with data processing goes back as far as 1930, at which time the company made widespread use of tabulating equipment and electromechanical analog computers. Later, first-generation computers, such as the IBM 650, replaced the tabulating equipment.

The first true computers were introduced in 1954 by scientists at one of the company's advanced technical and manufacturing centers for use in the design and development of an advanced and complex engine. In the same year some business systems were trans-ferred to a Univac, which had been installed at one of the major consumer manufacturing complexes. While the computer in the scientific area yielded the hoped-for results, the benefits anticipated from the business systems computer were not fully realized.

During the next ten years computers flourished throughout the organization. Initially, the various computer units operated independently of one another, but eventually the responsibility for both financial and scientific computers was assigned to the financial organization. The scientific group, however, retained its programmers and, in a few instances, some computers. Also, one large plant complex developed its own computer language, so its computer could handle both financial and scientific data. Currently, 95 percent of the computer complexes throughout the company report to the financial function.

Computer operations at the corporate level are centralized under accounting services and report to the controller (see Exhibit B). During the past five years, however, top management has weighed possible future locations, considering especially the potential leverage offered by the new third-generation computers. The overriding objective is to achieve the most effective operational utilization of both the computer and the facilities needed for a companywide management information system.

Several alternatives for structuring the computer complex have been examined, including organizing it on a geographic basis, relating it to a customer base, and aligning it with the major product groups. Under any of these alternatives the corporate computer complex would maintain its present coordinative and control function.

Underlying the final location decision is the need for management information to keep pace with the corporation's plans to double its business every ten years. This planned rate of growth anticipates continued expansion of product division operations throughout the country, the introduction of new products and related operations, and the correlation of data in a comprehensive management information system.

The corporate computer staff foresees the day when the entire computer complex will be located at headquarters and will function as a time-sharing service bureau, with all users having remote terminals and consoles tied to the central location through telecommunications. A major factor in the success of such a computer complex would be the cost and reliability of data transmission.

The company distinguishes between management information systems and operational systems, including in the management information systems, operations research and such long-range considerations as business planning, research and development planning, product planning, policy plans, and measurement; operational systems, on the other hand, are concerned with ongoing, day-to-day activities, such as sales and manufacturing.

The corporate computer office receives vast amounts of input data about operations, but because of the decentralized organizational structure of the company, information retrieval is on a divisional rather than an overall basis. However, the company is moving to the integration of systems for each product group, which it hopes eventually will develop into a comprehensive management information system. Already, the company has a series of programs that enables top management to determine the state of business worldwide, evaluate key areas, and analyze product-line and financial results.

Considerable work has been done with simulation, but primarily it has been related to operational areas and decision-making situations. Considerable effort has also been made to educate managerial and technical personnel in understanding the capability and uses of the computer. As part of these efforts a series of mathematics-appreciation courses has been designed, which includes elementary mathematics as well as modeling and simulation techniques. To date, 4,000 employees have participated in the courses, and from the requests for additional courses, it appears that the results have been favorable. Computer education for management has also been encouraged by including study of computerization in the company's formal management development programs.

Case 3:
International Petroleum and Petrochemical Company

This company, with several substantial operating subsidiaries, is organized on a geographic basis. Subsidiary companies and such functions as marketing and accounting are directed on a regional basis. Functional staff guidance is provided from corporate headquarters, but the subsidiaries are highly autonomous. The company has a strong research and development capability.

A major thrust for the company's advancement in the use of EDP equipment came from its R&D people who early in the 1950's seized on the computer as a means of furthering their laboratory-research effort. The subsidiary companies also began to use computers in the operation of their refineries. Historical production data, accounting reports, and other documents for refinery management were prepared for processing on the computer at each location.

As the various units in the field began to turn to EDP and to acquire their own computer equipment, considerable overlap resulted, not only in computer facilities but in systems, in programs, and in the data generated. The growing costs of this duplication became apparent, leading to a study that revealed the need for stronger central control of all aspects of computer usage. Moreover, top management realized that the company would have to develop a broad management information system in the near future.

For a time, management considered assigning responsibility for the management information function to the corporate R&D unit, since many R&D employees had become fairly knowledgeable about EDP applications in the research area. The other alternative was to assign the coordinating role to an existing staff function at headquarters—in particular, finance. The question was finally resolved, by the chief executive, in favor of the financial function. He feared that if the task of developing the company's EDP system were assigned to R&D, the unit's highly successful research activities might suffer.

The transfer of responsibility from the field units to headquarters was not accomplished overnight. As late as 1965 there were 35 computers (mostly IBM 1401's) in company locations across the country, and all but five were tied by communication links to a large IBM 7094 II and 360 complex in the headquarters city. A cadre of EDP personnel had developed around each computer in the field, and in nearly every case there appeared to be a genuine need for some computer capability at these locations.

By 1967 the number of computers had risen from 35 to 42, with an increase in rentals of some $260,000 a year. This additional equipment was installed in line with a carefully developed plan through which the company hoped to attain greater flexibility and increased capacity. It was felt that the ultimate advantages of the new alignment, which included a greater variety of equipment (Honeywell 200's, SDS 930's, IBM 360's in various models, and GE equipment), would far outstrip the increase in rental costs once the necessary reprogramming was accomplished. The company's basic goal continued to be the strengthening of corporate control over all EDP operations as a means of achieving greater uniformity in systems and program configuration and more emphasis on the generation of information useful on a companywide basis.

At the corporate level, responsibility for the computer complex is lodged in the corporate controller's department (see Exhibit C). As the company moved toward centralization, changes were made in the organization of the department in order to facilitate overall company control of EDP operations. The assistant controller, who is in immediate charge of the EDP operation, was formerly responsible for (1) accounting policy, (2) the computer center at corporate headquarters, and (3) organization and methods. As Exhibit D shows, his responsibilities now revolve exclusively around EDP and the functions that depend on EDP—systems design and operations research.

The organization chart and the listing of the assistant controller's responsibilities

EXHIBIT C. *Location of the Corporate Computer Complex*

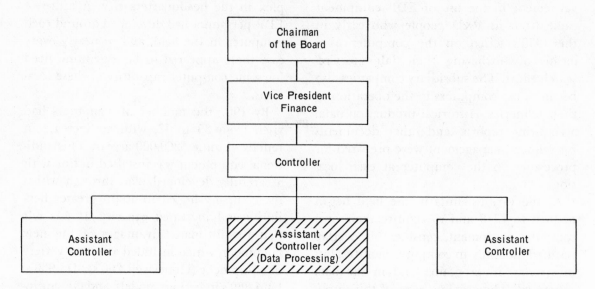

tell only part of the story. Not all of the systems development people, not all of the programmers, and not all of the EDP equipment are at present within the assistant controller's immediate ambit.

Because of the legacy of local autonomy in computer operations and the continued need for computers in the field, it was not considered feasible to bring all EDP personnel and functions into corporate headquarters. At various company locations, there are still more than 100 systems development people and many more programming and maintenance people who continue to develop systems and to program, operate, and maintain the equipment and programs for their own local operations. But guidance and direction from corporate headquarters are much closer than before. Technologically, there are also closer ties between headquarters and the field. A series of IBM 360–65's in the corporate headquarters is connected directly by telecommunication with computers in nine locations in the field and by direct input with three locations in the headquarters city. Even closer ties between the field and headquarters locations are planned.

All of this means that companywide congruity of equipment, systems, and programs has taken on greater importance. As mentioned, the achievement of this is now the responsibility of the corporate controller. Specifically within his purview are data processing applications that involve six man-months or more to develop, equipment expenditures if they entail a monthly rental of $1,250 or more or a capital asset value of $50,000 or more, and use by subsidiary companies of outside computer consultants and of computer or programming services.

Aside from these specific instances of direct control, the corporate controller, through the assistant controller and his staff, relies on the traditional company concept, shared by other staff units, of achieving the desired coordination through consultation. The corporation's long-range data processing objectives and the general outlines for attaining these objectives are worked out cooperatively by the subsidiary companies (or other corporate departments) and the assistant controller and his staff. Within this framework the subsidiary companies devise plans for systems development, data processing applications, operations research, sched-

EXHIBIT D. *Organization of Corporate Data Processing Function*

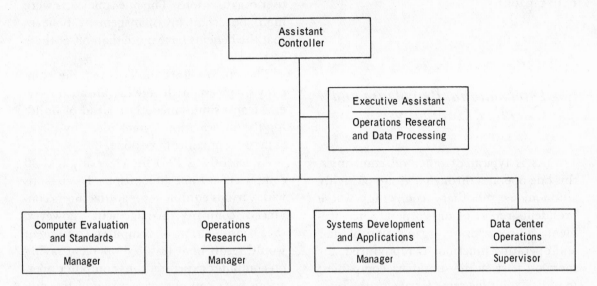

ules, equipment acquisition, and personnel requirements. They receive assistance in the design of new systems, in the exploration of applications, in the evaluation of the cost-benefit aspects of proposed applications, and in the determination of manpower and dollar requirements of proposed plans.

The corporate controller initiates projects in the subsidiary companies in order to generate needed companywide data, and data processing personnel in the subsidiaries are expected to work closely with their counterparts at the corporate level. It is necessary, of course, for the subsidiaries to adhere to standards, established by the corporate controller, for programming and hardware configuration. These standards are maintained through periodic reviews of data processing activities in the subsidiary companies.

At this time the company uses EDP equipment mainly for "technical" and "data processing" purposes. As mentioned earlier, computers are used extensively in the operation of refineries, where a great deal has been done with simulation. These applications, in conjunction with R&D uses, account for most of the *technical* usage within the company. Accounting applications now use the bulk of *data processing* computer time, which aggregates approximately three-fourths of the equipment's total running time and two-thirds of the rental costs.

The company is moving more deeply into the area of operations research, which it defines as research in all aspects of the business other than those related to physical processes. As the evolution of the company's information system progresses, and as broader data processing applications are developed, the proportion of data processing usage for fairly standard accounting purposes is expected to dwindle.

This company has neither completely centralized nor completely decentralized its computer facilities or the responsibility for their use. It maintains systems development, programming, and equipment operation and maintenance capabilities in both its field units and its corporate headquarters. But the extent of coordination and control exercised by the corporate staff in the corporate controller's department is increasing the centralization of responsibility for EDP activities. Future moves toward centralization will be taken in light of continuing needs of the field units for some form of EDP capability.

Case 4:
International Petroleum and Chemical Company

As is typical of other oil companies, this one operates through a group of highly autonomous subsidiary companies whose presidents report to top corporate management. The corporate organization of staff and operating functions is reproduced, for the most part, in the subsidiary companies; to some extent the same is true for the computer complex.

When corporate management decided, in 1965, to develop a consolidated information system, it established task groups in marketing, manufacturing, supply and transportation, and administration (largely accounting and control) to undertake the initial survey work in their respective areas. Computer applications related to personnel information were developed by the corporate employee relations staff.

A typical task force was composed of a director, a representative of the equipment manufacturer (who served as technical expert and design engineer), and representatives from various activities of the functional or operating unit. Overall, some 500 senior, topflight people in the company participated in the task-force studies—and 200 of them were involved full time for six months. Subsequently, the task forces were replaced by permanent data systems development committees that decided on the applications needed in specific areas. This approach, coupled with a massive program of conversion to third-generation computers, was an attempt to involve operating people in the development of an information sys-

tem that could serve the precise needs of user organizations. The one-time costs were high, but company management believes that the benefits have more than offset these costs.

The entire effort underscored the company's concern with moving ahead on several fronts simultaneously instead of building the information system piece by piece, as many companies have done.

As recently as 1964 the company had 40 computers at some 30 locations. Discussions with various equipment manufacturers convinced company management, however, that consolidation of computer equipment would result in at least a 30 percent saving on computer expenses; thus computer operations were consolidated in two of the subsidiary companies.

Progress was slow in reaping the benefits of this consolidation; finally, as the third-generation computers were introduced, one person was designated as head, at the corporate level, of a data systems planning staff and was assigned responsibility for spearheading the development of a consolidated information system based on use of third-generation computers. The company's top management considered the appointment necessary in order to get the EDP effort off dead center.

Each of the two major computer installations in the company serves the subsidiary in which it is located as well as other subsidiaries in the same geographical area. These installations offer hardware capability, programming services, and technical assistance to user organizations within the subsidiary companies they serve; systems development and design are carried out in various operating departments within the subsidiary companies. Since there is no computer facility at headquarters, one of the installations also serves corporate informational needs. Both subsidiary facilities have IBM 360 equipment.

EXHIBIT E. *Organization of an Electronic Data Processing Department*

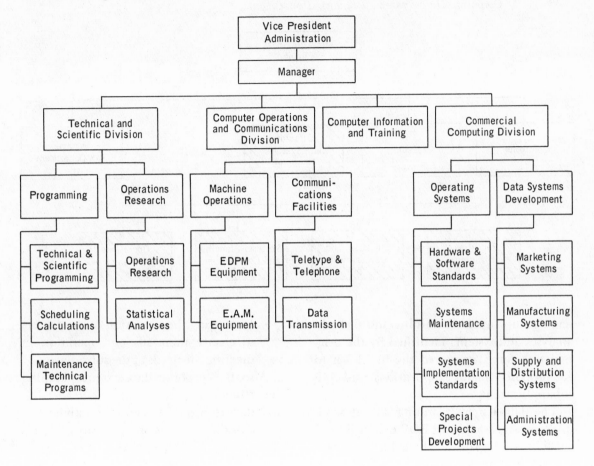

The two computer complexes are organized along similar lines. In one of the subsidiaries, however, the computer organization reports to the general manager of administration; in the other, to the vice president, administration. Exhibit E shows the structure of one of the complexes and its reporting relationships. The organization of the corporate data systems planning department is shown in Exhibit F.

Working closely with the corporate EDP staff, each center has two primary objectives:

- To attain standardization of computer input from the subsidiaries it serves and to work with these subsidiaries in determining the form of output.

- To develop applications to meet the

needs of the subsidiary in which the computer center is located.

As noted, emphasis was placed at the outset on developing information systems in four areas: marketing, manufacturing, supply and transportation, and administration. In all the functional units in each of the subsidiary companies there are permanent data systems development groups. These groups evolved from the task forces that took part in the initial developmental efforts, and they are organized along the same lines. They design systems and the related applications. In some instances, the original task forces' ideas have had to be adapted to uses that can be made operational in a short time and that show an immediate benefit. In one subsidiary, for example, the marketing sys-

EXHIBIT F. *Organizational Relationships and Structure of the Corporate Data Systems Planning Department*

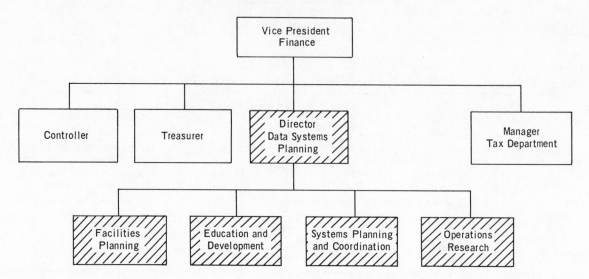

tems group, upon examining the 600-odd analyses and systems identified by the original task force, narrowed the list down to 15 proposed major applications and 119 subapplications.

The data systems planning staff at headquarters acts as resident EDP expert for the subsidiary companies, which turn to it for counsel and advice in the development of their systems. In addition, the corporate group plays a direct role in the subsidiaries' EDP operations by:

- Achieving compatibility among computer facilities and avoiding duplication in equipment and developmental efforts by (1) advising the subsidiary computer centers and managements on all hardware proposed for installation, either in the centers or at terminal locations, and (2) coordinating and approving all software changes.
- Maintaining a manual of operating systems and application standards, and reviewing and approving additional standards developed by the centers.
- Consulting with subsidiaries regarding software.

- Reviewing the operation of the centers to ensure their efficient operation in meeting the needs of the subsidiaries.

Also, the corporate data systems planning department is responsible for leadership and direction of the planning activities of the subsidiary data systems groups, for coordination of all computer and telecommunications systems operations, and for formulation of overall corporate policies and objectives governing both short- and long-term computer activities. The corporate group does not have authority over the subsidiary groups—each subsidiary, in developing its systems, is responsible for ensuring that the systems are compatible with others in the company.

Companywide coordination in systems development is accomplished in four ways:

- Though the reviews and approvals described above.
- Through a number of coordinating groups headed by corporate EDP personnel and composed of representatives from the subsidiaries.
- Through two groups chaired by the corporate director of data systems plan-

ning and established expressly to exchange information on various elements of the information system.

- Through the assignment to each of the two computer centers of corporate data systems personnel who resolve systems anomalies and duplications, or if they cannot be resolved at the subsidiary level, call discrepancies to the attention of the corporate systems director.

For some time, various subsidiaries within this corporation have been using operating models in making decisions. Under the present coordinated approach to EDP, a small corporate staff group is working with a committee of representatives from each of the subsidiaries to devise a consolidated model for short-term operations planning, as opposed to long-term capital or financial planning. With this model, operations planning will be related to profit-and-loss data from the subsidiaries, and subsidiary managements and departments can adapt their tactics to the overall strategy determined.

The corporate staff working on the consolidated operations planning model is intensely interested in the development of a corporate information system and in attaining uniformity in the subsidiaries' inputs into the system. The subsidiary models used in the corporate model are, in some cases, quite complex. One subsidiary, for example, has a model with 4,000 equations and 6,000 variables. Moreover, in some subsidiaries there are both tactical and strategic models, as well as combination models.

Another corporate department has responsibility for long-range (ten-year) financial and economic planning. While some simulation is done, the lack of internal feedback inhibits any modeling at the present time; but the department is in the process of converting to an IBM 360 program, which will enable it to engage in corporate simulation aimed at developing or revealing new relationships in data for use both in planning and in variance and probability analysis for control purposes.

In essence, the company has elected to implement a comprehensive information system all at once. Although its subsidiaries have used many fairly sophisticated information systems for some time, through headquarters guidance each has drastically revised its concept of an information system by examining minutely the needs of its major functional units. A significant proportion of the corporation's middle management has thus been involved in systems planning, which has been closely related to operating needs. This approach, in the opinion of company management, is providing data on which to build corporate models for advanced planning much sooner than if the company had adopted the function-by-function or subsidiary-by-subsidiary approach to systems development.

Case 5: *Public Utility*

The company manufactures electricity, gas, and steam, and markets these products, as well as electric and gas appliances, in a multistate territory. It is a member of a regional electrical interconnection system and belongs also to a consortium of utility companies sponsoring development of a nuclear-powered electrical manufacturing facility.

Organizationally, the company is centralized. The executive offices of chairman and president are supplemented by a management group largely consisting of company officers who head up functional divisions. At present, the company is engaged in restructuring its organization to reduce the number of organizational layers and to direct decision-making responsibilities to lower organizational levels.

The computer was first introduced into the financial division, because tabulating equipment could not handle the increasing volume of financial and accounting data. In 1962, after a two - and - one - half year study, the company acquired an IBM 7070. The first program was designed for processing customer-account billings, and the conversion was undertaken on the theory that both the computer and the tabulating equipment would be used in parallel to process data. Because of a need for extensive "debugging," the original estimate of three months for conversion was extended to one year, and an IBM 7074 eventually replaced the 7070.

The resources of the original computer complex were divided between the processing of financial and accounting data and the auditing control system. Large clerical recordkeeping activities were identified, and systems were developed for computerizing these areas. Because the financial division did not want to dilute the resources of the computer organization by attempting to undertake too many diverse projects, priority was assigned to those activities involving financial and accounting data. Once the bulk of these data was computerized, the needs of other functional areas would be considered. At this stage, cost savings and speed in processing were the goals of the computer organization.

Although attention has focused primarily on the development and application of accounting programs, the computer organization also undertook the development of some programs not directly related to accounting in response to pressure from other functional groups. At present, the company payroll is being converted from tabulating equipment to the computer; not only will this program supply salary information for work measurement studies, but it will begin the development of an overall personnel data base covering all employees.

Seeing the computer's potential in the technical area, the engineering division sought to use the financial division's computer for certain engineering projects, but the needed computer time was not available. Therefore, the engineering division acquired its own computer, a 1620, which was more suited to technical data processing. At first, the engineering division preferred to use the systems and programming personnel assigned to the financial unit. But they were unavailable, and consequently, engineering had to develop a total computer operations organization to service its needs. (Despite the difficulty of establishing and maintaining a special computer operations, engineering's EDP staff is, in general, more sophisticated than that of the financial unit.)

Exhibit G shows the present organizational location of computer activities in the two functional divisions of finance and accounting, and engineering. The activities in the accounting division are totally involved with business data related to financial and accounting information and control. In the engineering division, computer activities focus primarily on technical and scientific problems—electric-load forecasting, research and electrical systems planning, and interconnection planning.

The capability of engineering's computer operations has expanded beyond engineering functions as other divisions, unable to receive service from the financial computer, have turned to engineering for service. Customers are not charged for service; all costs are borne by the computer operations unit. The computer group establishes priorities for allocation of personnel and machine time, but as a result of the number of engineering and other applications, the assignment of priorities is somewhat complex.

There is a clearcut need to enlarge the engineering computer capacity, but high

EXHIBIT G. *Organizational Location of Computer Operations*

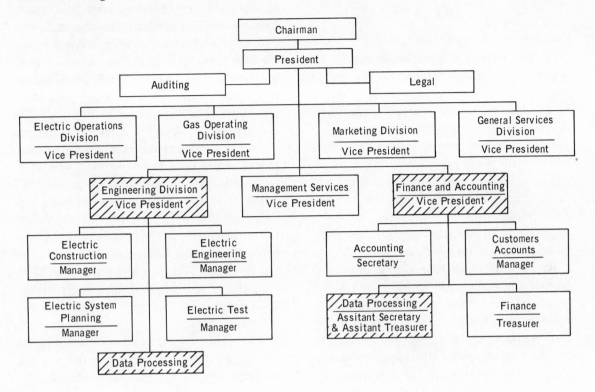

turnover among computer personnel has limited such expansion. Some company units, not being able to obtain time on internal computer operations, are using outside computer service bureaus.

Top management clearly recognizes the potential of the computer, beyond its use as a processor of financial and accounting data, and the dangers and inefficiencies of uncoordinated computer operations. Early in 1966 the chief executive officer set in motion the first efforts toward determining overall company needs and the most efficient means of serving all divisions. These steps were followed in 1967 by the assignment of the following corporate responsibilities to the auditing division:

To develop, in conjunction with representatives of management and the staff services division and representatives of other divisions, a plan for a long-range study to re-

solve the best internal organization for achieving expanding computer applications; to determine what type of installation would be feasible and economical for all data processing requirements; to determine whether the various systems and methods of activities now being performed throughout the company, including the systems design and programming functions of the present data processing department, should be brought together into a single systems and procedures unit; and [to determine] to what extent, if any, the audit function should be related to a centralized computer organization unit.

Overall, the company's EDP operations are in a transitional phase. They are moving from being uncoordinated and independent operations to the point at which the need for dual equipment and computer organizations is being carefully evaluated.

Case 6:
Public Utility

The company is an amalgamation of public-utility operating companies spread throughout a wide section of the United States, but with each company operating in its own geographic area. Among these companies is one which transmits natural and manufactured gas.

The corporate staff provides guidance to the operating companies in specialized areas and handles much of the reporting work required by governmental agencies regulating the companies' businesses.

Responsibility for EDP has never existed outside the accounting function. This fact points up the conviction of company management that EDP is most beneficial in the accounting area.

The first major EDP application was customer accounting—the area in which the largest immediate savings could be realized. The initial system was on punched cards and was developed individually for each of the operating companies. In 1957 the punched cards were replaced by corporate-wide use of the IBM 650 system, which did both addressing and billing. Subsequently, customer accounting was converted to an IBM 7074, at which time shareholder accounts were also transferred to the 7074. Updating was done daily, using NCR equipment.

It is the company's policy to move cautiously into new areas of EDP use. The tendency of some EDP-oriented people to act too quickly is tempered by general management's control over the applications actually used. The general policy is that only management knows what should go into the computer and what should come out.

The computer is regarded solely as a management tool and EDP as a service function. It is considered unnecessary, indeed unwise, to have EDP report to the chairman as a separate function. First, this would increase the already heavy managerial burden on the chairman and possibly impair the effectiveness of both functions; second, the necessity of making EDP decisions at this level would result in delay and in a great deal of "wheelspinning."

All company business-oriented activities —systems development, programming, computer operations, planning, and the like —which constitute most of the data processing done in the company, are the responsibility of the corporate vice president of accounting, who is also the corporate treasurer. This functional area is charted in Exhibit H. In addition, there are some EDP activities oriented to R&D and engineering, and responsibility for them lies within these functional areas.

The company view is that the responsibility for the computer should not be assigned necessarily to the "best suited" person, but that the location of this responsibility should be determined by the computer's use. Since nearly every operation of the corporation requires some report, which must be filed with a regulatory agency, and in view of the history of the computer's development within the company, it is considered highly unlikely that responsibility for the major core of EDP activities will be moved out of accounting in the near future.

The central computer installation, devoted to business applications, is in an area far removed geographically from corporate headquarters, but it is fairly near most of the operating locations. The installation is connected by microwave and leased-line telecommunications with 200 input/output terminals in the seven states in which gas is retailed by the operating companies. The communications network utilizes facilities that are under the direction of the operations function. The R&D, engineering, and other operating uses of EDP are separate

EXHIBIT H. *Location of Computer Unit*

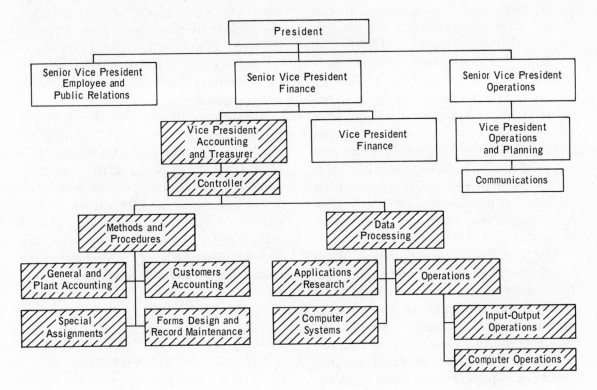

from the central business computer installation.

Most of the present EDP-based business systems are corporatewide. The company's success in attaining these broad applications stems from the close guidance provided the operating companies by the accounting vice president and the members of his staff, who have worked diligently to mesh systems in the operating companies with overall corporate systems.

The corporate EDP group believes strongly in the "total systems" concept, and as the company has moved toward this objective, the corporate staff's part in EDP planning and implementation has become increasingly stronger. For example, practically all of the EDP people in the company are assigned to the accounting vice president's area of responsibility.

Exhibit H shows how the procedural aspects of EDP are separated from data proc-

essing operations. The director of methods and procedures has a standard methods and procedures unit, as well as another group that evaluates the feasibility of proposed EDP applications. The methods and procedures group, and not the EDP staff or the user organization, is responsible for determining and defending the use of EDP in specific instances. One of the group's major concerns is to match the job with the machine in order to avoid applying too much machine to a relatively minor job.

Actual hardware acquisition is also the responsibility of the vice president of accounting. He acquires those computers that he believes will most efficiently and effectively achieve the EDP goals determined by a high-level corporate policy committee. No computer acquisition is carried out by the operating companies.

The major computer applications are customer accounting, stockholder records—

issuance of dividend checks, proxies, and proxy follow-ups—daily updating of customers' accounts receivable, some accounting uses tied to gas meters, and billings to wholesale customers. Most of the customer-account programs are real time, so that customers raising questions can be answered immediately. This means that the computer equipment must be available for queries during the day; thus the remaining accounting programs are processed overnight, with the central unit receiving the input from outlying locations during the day, processing it, and transmitting the output during the night.

The payroll also is computerized, as are various forms of material and supply controls and work equipment data. And the company uses the computer for budgeting on the basis of its estimates of past and future energy requirements. These data are programmed in substantial detail and in a variety of forms and are updated regularly. Actually, only a portion of the budgeting process is now computerized, but efforts are being made to create a computer data base that will serve as the basis for all budgeting.

Despite the emphasis on cost control inherent in his position, the vice president of accounting has avoided justifying a computer or its application on the basis of cost savings alone. The philosophy is "Let's get the equipment to do the job we know needs doing, and then we'll see about the cost savings." Cost, of course, is a factor, but the company management believes that other considerations, such as contribution to the ability to make better business decisions, are more important.

In a broad sense the company's top management has a clear appreciation of what EDP can do in the accounting and control function. Its acceptance at other levels has been slower. While it is recognized that a management-education program is needed to show managers in different functions

what the computer can do, this task has been left largely to the vendors. Overall, the general allusions to EDP capability in the vice president of accounting's reports to the management committee have been the only attempts to acquaint management with EDP potential.

An incident illustrating the need for broader computer education occurred recently when top management, for the first time, asked for a specific EDP application —the computerization of employee benefits. Since there were no EDP experts in employee relations and no employee relations experts in EDP, several employee relations people had to be enrolled in a vendor's EDP course in order to fulfill this demand.

Case 7:
Insurance Company

The company is organized around several functional divisions and two major profit-center divisions—one including individual life and annuities, and the other, group insurance and group pensions. The data processing function reports to a senior vice president who is also responsible for personnel, public relations, advertising, and sales promotion. The structure of the present data processing department is shown in Exhibit I.

The company has used punched cards and tabulating equipment since 1920. The first computer, an IBM 650, was introduced by the actuary and controller to replace tabulating equipment, and its primary users were claims and payroll and the actuary department (the actuary department also serviced other units of the company).

In the late 1950's a study group was formed to assess the potential value of the computer to the company as a whole and the desirability of organizing the EDP func-

EXHIBIT I. *Organizational Location and Structure of the Data Processing Department*

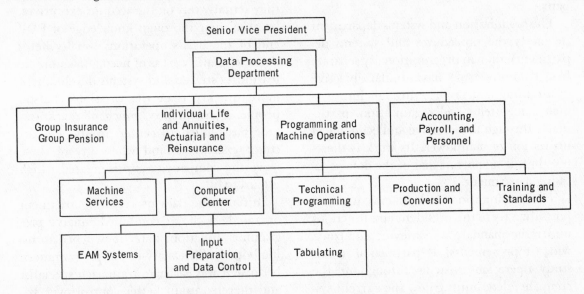

tion as a separate unit. The group's first work was a feasibility study of computer applications to the group division. As a result of this study, a new computer was acquired in 1959, and an independent data processing department was organized.

The new department was staffed by personnel from the data processing group in the actuary department and the team which had participated in the feasibility study. Some consideration was given to merging the existing systems and procedures department with the new data processing unit, but top management decided against this, fearing that the data processing function might dominate systems and procedures development; also, plans were being made to enlarge the scope of the systems and procedures function to encompass organization planning.

To ensure that the data processing department would operate solely as a service unit and that it would not interfere in the operations of the divisions, management emphasized at the outset that the user organizations themselves would determine whether or not to use the department's data processing services. Thus the initial task of

the new department was to attract prospective customers; it could persuade a potential user to undertake a feasibility study, but the final decision on whether to adopt or reject a proposed system rested with the user organization—and regardless of its decision the user had to pay for the costs incurred.

In the beginning, user organizations knew very little about applying the computer to their operations; therefore, many of the applications and programs developed were, in practice, actually determined by the data processing department. As time passed, however, the user organizations developed liaison personnel who knew the computer and could identify the areas in their units in which EDP could be used to advantage. The basic function of these people was to define the problem and set the specifications.

The company's initial objective in using the computer was to achieve cost savings by reducing staff; later, cost savings in operations became a major goal. For some of the programs developed, the resulting cost savings could not be documented, but these programs were adopted on the basis of the contributions they would make to the company.

The organization and systems department (formerly the procedures and systems department), though organizationally separate from data processing, has a similar objective of attaining cost savings through improvements in systems and organization, particularly through the effective and economical utilization of manpower. Its work is therefore in full support of that of the data processing department.

The organization and systems unit reports directly to the president and functions under the mandate of achieving company-wide improvements. Departmental teams study operations systems throughout the company, determining how the current system can be improved, if it is suitable for EDP, and if EDP would effect greater savings than a noncomputerized system. Systems that would benefit from EDP are turned over to the data processing department for a more detailed feasibility study and for recommendation to users.

Overall, the role of the organization and systems department is long-range organization planning—the most effective utilization of manpower—and systems improvement and EDP are vital steps in working toward this goal. The long-range organizational planning that is done by the department is tied in with the long-range corporate business planning that is carried out in the actuary's department.

The data processing department coordinates its work for the major divisions through a staff of account executives responsible for collaborating with specific users on determining the feasibility of a proposed application and on developing approved systems; the account executives then turn the work over to programmers in their department who actually develop the programs.

Although user groups are expected, in

principle, to prepare their own systems, they actually rely on the account executives, because their thorough knowledge of EDP and of the user's operations usually helps them to identify areas of need and complete feasibility studies and systems development more quickly than the division's liaison people. Consequently, much of the know-how has tended to center around key account executives, and when any of these leave the company, a gap is created which is hard to fill.

Initially the data processing department operated with a combined analyst-programmer function. Later it switched to using both systems analysts and programmers, because it was easier to train each specialist and thereby attain better control over systems development and program development.

Over the years, top management's desire for, and emphasis on, cost savings has been communicated rather forcefully to the user organizations. In addition the annual budgets are reviewed by top management to ascertain that sufficient funds have been allocated to EDP development. Thus division and department heads must have sound reasons for not using EDP.

At present the emphasis is on cost-saving applications for various operations. But the data processing department is aware of the value of a comprehensive management information system and is attempting to develop data bases for the operations systems so that eventually they can be integrated into a comprehensive system.

A little work has been done in simulation, primarily in the corporate income tax area. Different tax situations have been projected, and on the basis of long-range projections and possibilities, attempts have been made to simulate a model corporate office.

Although the personnel relations and data processing departments report to the same senior vice president, very little has been done to develop EDP applications for the personnel function.

Computer education for management has been limited. Training efforts have been directed largely to user personnel directly involved with the data processing department, and these are generally at lower-management levels. In part, this reflects the emphasis on cost-saving operational applications. However, with increasing interest in developing a management information system and broader applications, computer education is appearing at higher levels. During the past year, most of the company's vice presidents attended some formal, outside, computer-education program.

Case 8:
Retail Organization

The company is composed of a number of highly autonomous subsidiary companies or divisions that operate their own stores. Many of these subsidiaries were formerly family-owned retailing companies and have long traditions associated with a particular grade of product and service. The importance of maintaining each subsidiary's distinct identity is recognized clearly at corporate headquarters and underlies most of the decisions in which centralizing any aspect of the corporation's operations is a consideration.

In line with the concept of decentralized management, the only reporting relationships, functional or direct, that exist between the subsidiary divisions and the corporate level are between the presidents of the subsidiaries and the corporate president. No executive below the divisional president level reports in any way to corporate headquarters, and the only directives

that emanate from the corporate group are from the president.

The home office exercises broad financial controls and provides services as requested by the local managements. Corporate management views its role as one of providing leadership for the total corporation and of motivating the management of the subsidiary companies. Its involvement in the affairs of the divisional companies is exercised through "control by exception" in the short run and through planning based on extrapolation from the past in the long run. This pattern of corporate-subsidiary relationships has been largely responsible for the direction in which the company's data processing and information system functions have developed.

In the mid-1950's a central merchandising organization to which the company belongs conducted a thorough study of potential computer applications among its member companies. Through their involvement in the study, many of the company's divisional management members became aware of the potential of the computer and pushed for its use in their stores. Some people in the divisions also actually participated in experimental programs.

By 1964 most of the divisions had proposed buying computers. Needing guidance in evaluating these proposals, corporate management brought in an individual with strong accounting and EDP experience to serve as a consultant to the divisions. He knew inventory-control methods, and he quickly learned more about merchandising. Observing that the techniques being successfully used by distributors and wholesalers were not being applied by subsidiary merchandisers, who tended to operate by "the seat of their pants," he decided that the most feasible solution was to centralize EDP operations in the headquarters city and to serve the subsidiaries from there. A staff was assembled and a simple inventory-control system, which told the buyer when and how much to buy, was programmed. The system was developed and perfected in one subsidiary then introduced into others. Some subsidiaries, which did not have computers of their own, were able to use the central computer by means of telecommunications and to receive the output on an overnight basis.

Since its installation the system has been re-examined twice a year, and each time it has been expanded. Additional applications have also been developed, largely in the subsidiaries, for accounts receivable and payable, payroll, and other functions.

Aside from these developments, the company, in 1959, took one of the most significant early EDP steps in the retailing field by devising a standardized accounts-receivable system, which it hoped would overcome the individualistic approach to accounts receivable then prevailing in merchandising organizations. Because this early work, done on the IBM 650 at one location and on the NCR 304 at another, was not completely successful, there was some hesitation on the part of many of the subsidiaries to adapt their methods and procedures to the computer. Nonetheless, the subsidiary managers recognized that computers would play a growing role in their future operations.

During the development of the inventory-control system, and while the divisions were seeking corporate approval for purchases or rental of computers, the computer operation reported to the vice president of research. Later, this man became an executive vice president, and when this occurred, an ex-merchandising executive was appointed to the newly established position of vice president of data processing and information services. However, because most of the EDP development was being carried out in the subsidiaries, this position was dissolved and the current reporting relationships established.

Computer capabilities exist in all of the major subsidiaries as well as at corporate headquarters. Most of the computer applications developed by the subsidiaries and by the corporate group focus on operations and, because of the nature of the retailing business, are concerned mainly with generating and processing information.

As shown in Exhibit J, the data processing/information systems function is headed at the corporate level by a director of EDP research, who reports to the vice president of market research; he, in turn, reports to the executive vice president, who is concerned primarily with the actual operations of the corporation's many stores. This alignment of the data processing function was chosen because market research is the department that supplies divisional management with information for improving store operations.

Within the subsidiaries the computer responsibility is found in any one of a number of places. In nine of the subsidiaries it is assigned to a treasurer, a vice president of finance, or a controller. In one subsidiary it rests with the vice president of administration and planning and in another with the vice president of sales.

Each subsidiary carries out EDP activities in the merchandising area. Applications specifically geared to merchandising are developed on the subsidiary's computer by a corporate merchandising information services group. This arrangement ensures sufficient attention to merchandising applications and is necessary, management believes, because the computer's location in the financial area in most of the subsidiaries has sometimes resulted in limiting the use of the computer for other than accounting needs.

A total of 286 people throughout the corporation are engaged directly in EDP work. Of these, 76 are systems analysts and programmers, 159 prepare input, and 51

EXHIBIT J. *Organizational Location of EDP Responsibility*

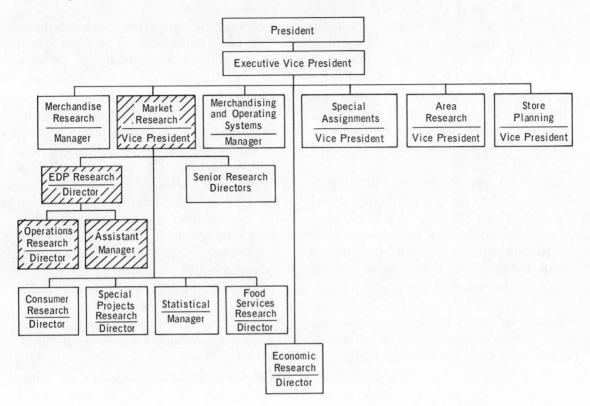

are computer operators. The corporate EDP group includes 22 people—19 in systems development, programming, and EDP management, and 3 in merchandising information services; in addition, there is a complement of computer and keypunch operators.

Two-thirds of those now engaged in EDP work were previously in some aspect of retailing; the remainder were recruited from outside the company, solely on the basis of their computer skills.

Because of the individual character of the subsidiaries, which is considered one of the corporation's basic strengths, most of the systems work is done in the subsidiaries. A central systems group to develop companywide systems is not considered feasible in view of the intricate balance of personal relationships within the subsidiaries, the informal but effective channels of communication that exist, and the large numbers of

people involved in developing and accepting a new system. In management's view it would not be realistic to send a systems team into a subsidiary for two to four months and expect that team to become well enough acquainted with the complexities of the subsidiary's business to successfully develop an effective system.

In keeping with the company's pattern of corporate-subsidiary relationships, the corporate director of EDP research does a great deal of advising for, and consulting with, the subsidiaries, but very little directing. He spends substantial time working with EDP managers in the various stores. He advises the corporate executive vice president on proposals from the subsidiaries for EDP programs and expenditures, and in rare instances he has participated in the recruitment and selection of EDP managers for individual stores.

The corporate EDP group works closely and in an advisory capacity with the merchandising information services group. In addition, a number of projects, primarily in the accounting area, have been undertaken jointly with subsidiaries. Here, too, the role of the corporate staff is an advisory one directed to ensuring that programs are uniform and that documentation standards are maintained at the same level in all of the participating subsidiaries.

The joint approach has three advantages: (1) The subsidiaries divide the effort and the cost; (2) sharing of experiences and ideas leads to development of better systems; (3) the subsidiaries learn from one another about better ways of approaching common problems of doing business.

Although the corporate aim is that the subsidiaries' applications will supply needed information for use at the corporate level, decisions on the final disposition of applications are made by the subsidiaries. If the subsidiary wants a system that will apply only to itself, then that is what is developed.

Currently, there are some applications that have been designed primarily to meet corporate information needs, but these are a small proportion of the total EDP effort. This is changing, however, as top management increasingly emphasizes the growing need for information of a total corporate nature. A study has been undertaken to determine how to generate such information while continuing to emphasize applications that meet subsidiary needs. This objective is being approached very carefully because there is some concern in the subsidiaries over the possibility of centralized computer activities. At present the corporate staff and top management do not believe that centralized data processing would be practicable, although they are considering a regional concept whereby a number of subsidiaries in the same geographic area would be linked together in their uses of the computer.

Most of the computer applications developed so far have been in accounting and merchandising. In the financial area each subsidiary has a team made up of the credit manager, the credit coordinator, the data processing manager, and a systems programmer working on ways to improve methods for extending credit by using the computer. The goal is to enable a salesclerk to check credit directly from the floor. Other accounting uses have been developed through the joint efforts described above. In all of these systems the individual subsidiary is responsible for operating and maintaining its own system.

Currently, there is very little in the subsidiaries in the way of management information systems, as such. However, because of the need for such a system at the corporate level, attempts are being made to educate subsidiary management to the value, for them and for corporate management, of a broad management information system. A two-part system is envisioned; it would be worked out in close conjunction with subsidiary management but would be developed at the corporate level to provide information on the entire corporation for use by corporate management, with some output going also to subsidiaries. Such a system will enable corporate management to analyze comparative data and ratios, identify exceptions and weak spots immediately, and take action to correct them. Plans call for data from the subsidiaries to be transmitted by telecommunications to corporate headquarters and to be added to the corporate data base.

Three goals have been established for the management information system:

- Determination of what information is needed and in what form, and the development of the system to meet these needs.

- Construction of a corporate profit model.
- Construction of a model for use in planning and forecasting activities that are now performed on manual business equipment but that could be handled more effectively through use of EDP. (One model is now in the development stage; it is designed to help the area-research and merchandising organizations determine the location and design of new stores.)

Like many companies, this one plans to do considerably more modeling in the future. At the moment the major drawback is a sufficiently extensive data base. And one of the objectives of the corporate staff's working with the divisions in the development of their information systems is to obtain additional data for this data base.

Despite the need to allay subsidiary managements' concern over the impact of possible centralization of EDP, almost nothing has been done by the corporate EDP staff to educate company executives to EDP uses. However, some executives have attended special schools and courses conducted by computer vendors. In addition the corporate director of EDP research has asked the employee relations department to set up a course, staffed by company executives in various areas of the retailing operation, to acquaint EDP people with how the company operates.

In summary, electronic data processing, which is relatively new, has focused primarily on the accounting, merchandising, and operational aspects of the business. Now the company is striving to construct a corporatewide information system to meet the needs of corporate management, while adhering to the basic tenet that the needs of the subsidiaries are paramount in the development of computer applications. In order to accomplish this, the approach has emphasized joint developmental efforts

among the subsidiaries. This requires a higher degree of uniformity than has previously existed and fosters close personal involvement by the corporate EDP staff in the developmental activities of the subsidiaries.

Case 9:
Electrical and Electronic Equipment Manufacturer

The company manufactures over 70 major types of electrical and electronic products. It is organized into a number of divisions which are combined under corporate group vice presidents on the basis of the products or functions involved.

Over 40 computer installations, utilizing a variety of equipment, exist within the corporation. The location of a computer complex within any division is at the discretion of the group vice president. As a result, throughout the divisions the responsibility for the installation is found in different locations, although by far the majority—approximately three-fourths—report to the divisional controller; the remaining one-fourth usually report to the plant manager, but sometimes to the general manager or to an operations manager. The computer complexes, in the divisions having computers, include the functions of systems development and programming as well as computer operations.

A corporate group under the director of management systems serves as a consultant to the divisions and controls introduction of specific EDP systems into the divisions. An elaborate telecommunications center, utilizing a variety of computer systems, also is operated under the overall direction of the director of management systems, who reports to the vice president, operations services. This relationship and the organ-

EXHIBIT K. *Organization of Corporate Level Computer Complex*

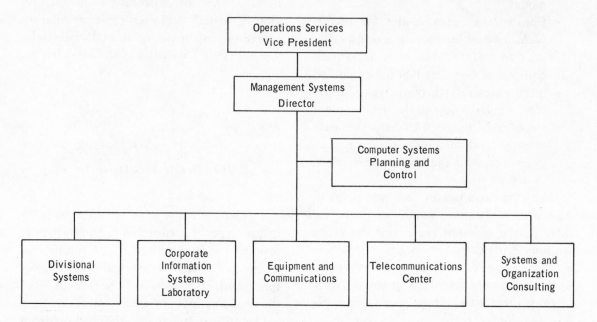

ization of the management systems department are shown in Exhibit K.

Aside from having overall responsibility for the acquisition of computer systems and the operation of the corporate computer center, the corporate management systems department serves as an information clearinghouse, and it participates with divisional systems people in systems development. The divisions learn from corporate headquarters of the latest and best systems in use within the company; each division is then in a better position to develop its own applications, with or without the aid of the corporate systems group, and yet still enjoy ready access to the experience and knowledge of other divisions. The corporate systems group maintains a current inventory of all running programs in the company as well as a record of what each division has done in systems development over the years. A management systems task force is now working with one division to develop a divisionwide management information system, which can serve as a future model for other divisions.

Through such efforts the management systems group is attempting to change two parameters in EDP operations within the divisions: (1) the state of the art, that is, how computer-based systems are used; and (2) the level of management participation.

In a company with numerous computer installations and a wide variety of equipment dispersed throughout its operations, expertise in EDP procedures alone does not result in effective systems. The management systems group therefore operates on the thesis that the key to attaining successful systems is to encourage divisional people to develop their own capabilities in the EDP area. It is believed that any instance of corporate control over the divisions, other than administration of computer acquisition and, to a degree, management development in the EDP area, would weaken the divisions' capability and autonomy in deciding how computers can be best used to serve their needs.

A breakdown of the company's total computer usage, in dollar percentages, works out approximately as follows: 25 percent for manufacturing purposes, 35 percent for engineering, 35 percent for accounting, and 5 percent for all other purposes. This is the overall corporate mix, and of course it varies in specific divisions. If there are any questions on desired applications of EDP within the divisions, representatives of the corporate group and divisional people jointly study the proposed application and make recommendations.

At the time of this study the corporate systems group was working to encourage division general managers to make further use of the computer for decision making in the following areas:

- *Organization* for getting the job done.
- *Systems* of bringing people together to accomplish the task and to provide for communications between them.
- *Staff* organization.

At one of the plants a substantial demonstration was developed to show that the computer can handle massive amounts of information, that it can and should be used to help make decisions in the three areas noted above, and that if a manager does not involve himself in using the computer for such decision making, someone else will take over the task.

Although the company is divisionalized, there is a clear tendency toward greater centralization of the information system and EDP operations functions. At the time of the study, corporate headquarters did approximately 20 percent of the EDP work in the company, and the divisions did 80 percent. There has been steady growth of computer applications both within the divisions and at the corporate level.

The corporate information systems group favors greater centralization of EDP operations, but it also appreciates that in the present company environment, the divisions hold the balance of power. Any moves toward centralization of EDP operations must therefore have the support of the divisions

and, in fact, should be initiated by them. It appears that divisional resistance to centralization of EDP operations is somewhat less strong in the area of information processing than it is in production uses for the computer.

There are indications that centralization of the computer operation will come about through the divisions' using the corporate computer center as a service bureau. A number of the divisions already have done this, but given the nature of this company, centralized processing will have to evolve. At its present level of development the computer center utilizes a CDC 6600 processing unit to receive and compile input data from various locations throughout the company. These data are either computerized at the center or switched to computers within a particular division for processing. Thus the center serves as a traffic policeman for the processing of information data for a number of divisions. Since a particular division may have only a few applications for a specific computer, it is generally not concerned with the type of computer that does the job. In fact, having part-time access to a computer lowers the cost for the division. Moreover, divisions can utilize the greater capability of the computers in the computer center for applications that would otherwise remain undone or that would require the division to install expensive equipment for which there might be only limited use.

The concept of terminal processing is that each division can treat the computer center as though it were its own facility and can trade off programs with other divisions. Although the corporate management systems group is not necessarily pushing for an interdivisional transfer of systems experience, the computer center encourages such an exchange since, increasingly, the divisions are feeling the burden of bearing the cost of systems development by themselves.

In the years ahead, through the exchange of systems among the divisions and the utilization of the centralized computer center, the processing of data in the company will become more highly centralized than it is today.

In attempting to service a number of divisions through one centralized computer system, the computer center staff encounters some problems in establishing the priority of requests from the divisions. The staff of the center attempts therefore to "balance the system" through an ideal plan under which the user division that pays, for example, 60 percent of the cost of the computer center budget will get 60 percent of the center's computer time. Within this broad framework the user divisions themselves determine their own order of priority and then convey the data to the computer center for processing.

Case 10:
Retail Company

The company operates on a nationwide basis with highly autonomous regional and individual-store profit centers, which are well supported by centralized functional service divisions. Although the profit centers' operations are autonomous, each is required to follow standardized corporate controls and procedures.

The history of data processing in the organization goes back to the early 1940's, when punched-card and tabulating operations were introduced, mainly in the controller's area. The basic company philosophy was that data processing could be adopted by any unit that could justify its use. The approach to data processing was informal and uncoordinated.

In 1962, through study of the computer's potential and its application to company-wide operations and requirements, the com-

pany found that an integrated data processing function was needed. As a result, a central corporate data processing department was established to coordinate all data processing throughout the company, including the evaluation, selection, and installation of computer hardware, and the development of systems, applications, standards, operational procedures, and research for the diverse functions of the company. Among the completed projects is the conversion of four different payroll systems into one corporate-wide system that takes account of the differing requirements of the states in which the company operates. Another example is the company's accounts-payable system, which is identical for each of the company's regional territories; a change in the system is sent to all regions to be put into effect.

The central data processing department reports to the vice president of operations. The computer installation in each of the regions is headed by a computer manager who reports directly to his regional vice president and functionally to the central data processing department, since the actual functioning of the regional installations is under the control of the central data processing department. Regional managements may request special programs, but their respective regional EDP managers must clear the programs with the central data processing department.

All regional computer hardware and software must be compatible with the corporate data processing configuration and must be approved by headquarters. The central data processing department also audits regional installations, evaluating the efficiency of computer utilization and the adherence to approved standards and practices. If a regional installation requires the assistance of an outside service bureau to supplement its capability, the central department handles the contract, so that the company benefits from group purchasing.

Charges for data processing activities are allocated to the user units (except for research and development), and these costs are absorbed into the central data processing department budget. This department also has the authority to determine the feasibility of programs and to establish priorities on the basis of the demands of the company as a whole and the companywide benefits of the program. For a sizable program the requesting unit completes a job authorization report outlining and justifying the program; if the suggested program is acceptable, the central department then makes a feasibility study and estimates costs. A simple noncontinuous program is handled and charged on a job-shop consulting basis.

Each of the major functional areas in the company has a liaison person who works with the central department. His role is to identify the major areas in his function that can be converted to data processing and to assist in the development of systems. Liaison individuals are selected jointly by the division and the central data processing department on the basis of their knowledge of the corporate function and their interest in, and aptitude for, data processing; knowledge of computer technology is regarded mainly as a matter of on-the-job development, supplemented by some formal training in computer concepts.

Although the liaison position is a temporary assignment, it is much sought after, since it represents a training ground and promotional step to higher levels of responsibility. After returning to his functional area, the liaison individual is usually in a good position to convey the concepts and value of data processing to his unit.

As part of its research and development effort, the central data processing department does model simulations of business operations. These are developed at operational installations and tested under actual conditions. The costs of all experimental research are charged to the central department until the system becomes operational; then the system becomes the property of the unit, which assumes the costs for the future.

The central department undertakes substantial training for both data processing and functional management personnel. A three-day seminar of general computer concepts is conducted for company officers and regional level management people. An additional abbreviated presentation of the computer data processing program is made to other management groups and internal management schools. Programs for data processing people are more intensive.

Though this company's original EDP philosophy was informal, it discovered that it needed a more integrated approach. So it developed its central data processing department to coordinate companywide EDP. For this company, centralization of data processing has proved a most effective approach.

Case 11:
Insurance Company

The company is decentralized, with three autonomous profit-center divisions —casualty, group, and life—reporting to the president, and four functional service departments—auditing, controller, financial, and management information and planning —reporting to the chairman.

The company tends to follow a centralized approach to computer operations. Accordingly, the responsibility for computer and data processing activities has been placed in an independent department, management information and planning (see Exhibit L). The relationship of computer services to overall company planning is recognized by the inclusion, within the de-

EXHIBIT L. *Organizational Location of the Corporate EDP Function*
(Management Information and Planning Department)

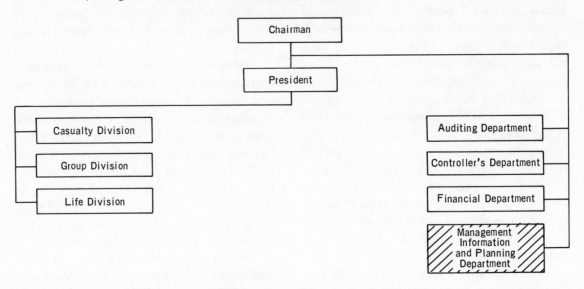

partment, of systems planning and the corporate planning and research functions.

Computerized data processing was introduced in the 1950's by the group division. The division's business activity had expanded rapidly, and it was faced with an increasing volume of administrative records to process. It was apparent, however, that it would be virtually impossible to recruit the number of clerical personnel needed, and that additional office space would not be available. Thus a computer seemed the best solution. The decision to acquire an IBM 705 was solely a divisional matter.

While waiting for delivery of the computer, a thorough systems analysis was undertaken, and an outside service bureau was utilized. During this period, internal systems and programs were also developed. In 1961 the first IBM 1401 was acquired, and a few years later a second 1401 was installed.

To the initial objectives of using the computer for speeding up clerical processing and cutting costs were added the development of new benefit programs and the provision of broader service to clients. At this

stage the computer, its personnel, and all data processing operations were the sole responsibility of the group division.

During 1961 and 1964 the casualty and life divisions also initiated computer feasibility studies. Corporate management was aware, however, of the operational and staffing inefficiencies that would eventually result from the uncoordinated operation of several computer installations. Therefore, it established a centralized computer services department in the controller's department, with the broad functions of providing electronic data processing facilities for the company as a whole, of developing systems, and of undertaking research and planning.

While centralizing the computer function, management realized that developing an effective companywide EDP operation would require a total effort on the part of the centralized computer services department and all the divisions. The computer services department and the divisions were therefore assigned specific responsibilities, as shown in Exhibit M. At the same time, top management established an advisory

EXHIBIT M. *Allocation of Responsibilities for Computer Operations Between the Central Computer Services Unit and Company Divisions*

Computer Services Department

1. Scheduling and operation of EDP equipment.
2. Output of EDP equipment.
3. Decisions regarding location of EDP equipment and site preparation.
4. Custody and library control of data processing tapes and other storage media.
5. Initial contacts with users and manufacturers.
6. Recommendations for acquisition of EDP equipment.
7. General research and development of advanced programming languages and techniques and multipurpose programming.
8. Establishment of technical standards for EDP machine usage, including programming standards.
9. Research, EDP systems analysis, and programming for all computer applications, except intradivision applications.
10. Technical advice to divisions when requested.
11. Maintenance of adequate liaison with user divisions.
12. Provision of facilities for education and technical training of EDP analysts, programmers, and operators.
13. Liaison with corporate long-range planning activities.
14. Preparation of cost estimates for proposed projects and reports of costs for completed and continuing projects.
15. Determination of EDP objectives for computer services department.
16. Preparation of computer services department budget.
17. Staffing to carry out the above responsibilities.

Divisions

1. Decisions regarding conversion of division functions or work to EDP and present applications needing modification.
2. Design, systems analysis, and programming of intradivision computer applications.
3. Determination of form, content, and disposition of EDP output.
4. Determination of intradivision priorities for use of computer time scheduled by the computer services department.
5. Training of division analysts and programmers.
6. Determination of EDP objectives for the division.
7. Short- and long-range EDP planning to achieve division objectives.
8. Systemization of data collection and data flow within the division.
9. Maintenance of liaison with the computer services department.
10. Staffing to carry out the above responsibilities.

committee, composed of senior management from each of the divisions. The purpose of the committee was to consider data processing problems and to evaluate the effectiveness of overall EDP operations.

Shortly after the formation of the computer services department, a centralized systems planning department was organized in the controller's division, with the responsibility, as implied in its title, for all noncomputer systems planning and applications. The systems planning and computer service departments were expected to coordinate with each other in determining the feasibility of computer applications in noncomputer systems.

In 1966 the computer services and the systems planning departments were transferred from the controller's division and in-

tegrated into a new functional unit, the management information and planning department, under a vice president reporting directly to the chairman (see Exhibit N). Thus for the first time all long-range planning and research functions and their related support activities were centralized in an independent unit. EDP responsibilities continued, however, to be carried out by the divisions and the computer services department, as outlined in Exhibit M.

Despite the establishment of the computer services department, the group division continues to operate its own computer. This is permitted because this computer is used almost exclusively for group division programs, and the computer operating personnel are thoroughly familiar with the division's business and its requirements.

EXHIBIT N. *Structure and Organizational Relationships of Computer Services Unit*

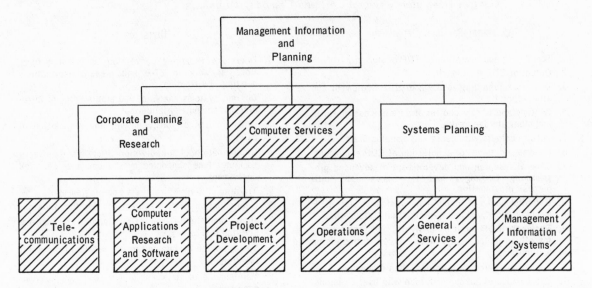

The computer services department oversees the operation, however, and can take advantage of unused computer capacity to process other applications. On the other hand, the life and casualty divisions use the hardware of the computer services department, though they have their own data processing personnel, and research, develop, and program their own applications. Thus each operating division has responsibility for its own computer personnel, for their selection and training, and for program development.

Since the primary role of the computer services department is to coordinate companywide EDP activities, it has the authority and responsibility for determining long-range EDP requirements for the entire company, for investigating and approving the purchase of new hardware, and for directing software research and applications and telecommunications. It also establishes standards, and while these are not imposed upon the divisions, they are generally accepted by them. Coordinative controls are effected primarily through regular meetings of key personnel of the computer services department and the divisional data processing sections.

In summary, the EDP activities in the company are in a transitional stage, but moving toward greater centralization, the objective being greater efficiency in providing more significant information to management and better and more rapid services to clients.

Underlying all these goals is the nature of the company's business, for though each operating division performs a unique service, all deal frequently with the same customers. Thus while data bases and applications are developed for the divisions' special needs, these data overlap to some degree.

Much of the effort of the computer services department now focuses on determining the minimum number of data-base files needed to meet the requirements of the separate divisions and of the company as a whole, while eliminating or minimizing overlapping programs. The ultimate goal is a broad companywide management information system that does not impinge upon the autonomy of any division in carrying out its own special type of operation.

Case 12:
Food Processing and Marketing Company

The company is organized along product lines; some divisions handle a variety of products, some a single item. In most respects the divisions operate autonomously, with little explicit direction from corporate headquarters. A few functions, however, are handled on a centralized basis. The information system, for example, and some plant accounting processes are centralized, which has permitted gradual centralization in the administration of the distribution function. Sales and production, however, as well as their support functions, continue to be decentralized, both divisionally and geographically.

A few years ago the operation of the company was considerably more centralized than it is today—reflecting the management style prevailing at that time. The change to a more divisionalized mode has more or less coincided with the development of the computer process within the company. Although company executives say that the change was not a direct result of the introduction of the computer, the implementation of decentralization was facilitated by the presence of the computer-based information system then being developed.

Originally, the computer activity was within the controller's office, under the vice president of finance, who was the first person in the company to fully appreciate EDP's potential for business and is the person who has shepherded the development of the EDP operation from the beginning. The function moved with him when he advanced to executive vice president. This was done to keep the activity under him rather than for organizational reasons. But until the computer operation became an independent department, it was always located somewhere in the financial and accounting activity, so that it had access to all divisions.

Most of the computer complex is located in the information systems department. This is a separate, centralized, corporate unit under the vice president of information systems. He reports to the executive vice president, whose functional responsibilities include most financial activities, corporate planning, and information systems. The location of the information systems function within the corporation is shown in Exhibit O.

Divisional headquarters in this company are situated in the same building as the corporate headquarters. All computers are located in the headquarters city, with the exception of a unit used to process invoices. Although the company has changed to a more decentralized mode of operation, the location of EDP equipment reflects greater centralization than existed ten years ago when there were computers at nine company locations across the country, doing mostly accounting work.

In part, this centralization results from using equipment that permits a single computer to do tasks formerly requiring more than one. It also reflects the growth of the information systems department and the need to control access to EDP equipment in order to govern costs of EDP applications throughout the company. As illustrated below, the company's method of relating the corporate EDP group to user divisions makes the centralization of equipment almost inevitable.

A key role in coordinating divisional EDP activities is played by the divisional liaison managers in each of the operating divisions. These men report directly to their divisional controller and indirectly and functionally to the vice president of information systems. The relationships of the divisional liaison manager to his division and to the information systems department

EXHIBIT O. *Organizational Location and Structure of the Information Systems Department*

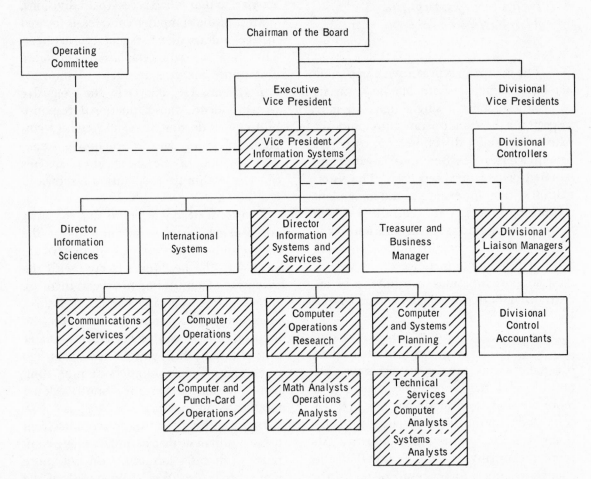

are illustrated by Exhibit O. The closeness of this relationship is indicated, in part, by the immediate proximity of the liaison offices to those of the information systems department management group.

In general, the liaison manager works with his own divisional people, using the knowledge of the computer that he has gained through his association with the corporate EDP group to determine what EDP applications his division needs. It is then up to the corporate information systems people to work with him in evaluating the feasibility of a proposed project, to establish priorities for the staff, and to estimate the computer time needed to implement the program. When the liaison manager con-

siders a potential application of EDP for his division, he must estimate the cost of doing the job and then justify it. In deriving this information, or at least some of it, he may lean heavily on the corporate information systems staff.

Divisional liaison men usually do not have a background in EDP when they are selected, but they must have been with their respective divisions for at least five years. To a large extent, liaison managers are considered by their superiors to be highly promotable, and the liaison function is viewed as an invaluable management training opportunity. Through training and continued close association with the corporate EDP group, the liaison men become well grounded in computer concepts and applications. Some develop great familiarity with the computers and become competent programmers. In short, the liaison manager, because of his experience in his division and his acquired knowledge of EDP, is in a position to interpret his division to the corporate information systems department and vice versa.

The information systems department operates as a "closed shop." This means that the departmental staff itself does the actual systems work, including programming, and that only this staff has access to the computer equipment. Although in addition to the liaison manager, many divisions have at least one man (usually in accounting) who does some detailed systems work himself, nearly all software design, systems programs, computer runs, and the like are performed by the corporate EDP staff.

Responsibility for operations research is centralized in the information systems department, but in some instances, operations research people are assigned by the department to the divisions in the hope that this will hasten the development of various operating models. This approach enables the systems staff to acquire from the divisions the detailed data needed for constructing models and provides the divisions with the assistance they need in implementing the models.

User divisions designate priorities within their own list of requests, but the corporate computer group decides how the time of systems-programmer personnel will be allocated, and assigns running time on the hardware itself. Potential conflicts have been somewhat forestalled by the practice, followed in recent years, of concentrating one year at a time on the problems of a single division and of giving this division first priority in systems development. In general, users are willing to accept the delays caused by this policy, because they either have had

"their year in the sun" or can look forward to a year when they will "own" the information systems department. Final decisions on the feasibility of a proposed EDP application are made by division heads, with advice from the corporate EDP group.

The acquisition of new hardware and the approval of new applications requested by user divisions are the responsibility of the corporate EDP group. Final decisions on new equipment are made by the executive vice president but are based on recommendations of the vice president of information services and his managers of computer operations, operations research, and computer and systems planning.

From its central position the corporate EDP group is able to evaluate company equipment needs and to determine the amount of computer time needed over a given period, the funds available for equipment purchase or rental, the types of equipment needed to perform the operations planned throughout the company, and the place within the company where the equipment can best be utilized. The ability to integrate equipment acquisition with planned applications is especially important in view of the computer group's role in determining priorities for the divisions seeking new computer programs.

Each division maintains a computer contol section, which receives data for input, edits and sends them to the computer, and evaluates output for acceptability. These units are staffed with divisional people who are aware of the division's interests in EDP activities at the computer center.

Operating costs for the information systems department, including expenditures for purchase or rental of data processing equipment, are shared by the divisions. Projects that are clearly for a specific division are charged directly to that division, but overhead and other indirect costs are apportioned among all the divisions. This sharing in overhead is an incentive to the divisions to use the EDP operation. At the same time, however, the system imposes monetary constraints, for the division must estimate one-time costs of applications, recurring costs, specific benefits to be derived, and the like. These estimates form the basis for calculation of the division's budget figures and its allocated share of the indirect costs.

Considerable work has been done with simulation. For example, two divisions have their entire operations on computerized models. The models indicate the impact of price changes in raw materials, changes in delivery items, price modifications by specific competitors, and a host of other factors. The models, of course, do not make decisions themselves, but through the development of discrete alternatives and Bayesian analysis, the basis of a decision becomes more explicit. A great deal of information of a historical and predictive nature is compiled for most of the company's operations, and a significant amount of this information is developed for, and made available to, top management.

In contrast to the sizable amount of EDP work that has been done in the operational areas of the company, little has been done in most of the so-called staff functions, with the exception of accounting.

The information systems department is now attempting to create a common data base that can be used by all divisions for a wide variety of applications. Because of this effort, a user division's request for EDP applications is weighed not only in terms of the application's immediate effectiveness but also in terms of its contribution to a common data base. For example, processing invoices on the computer is expensive compared to alternative methods, but the information derived is potentially useful for such applications as sales forecasting, production controls, and the like. Since this information is a byproduct of the EDP-generated invoices, the cost of obtaining the data is small compared to the advantages to be gained.

Case 13:
Diverse Heavy Equipment Manufacturer

In this highly divisionalized company the responsibility for all functions resides firmly with the divisions. Members of the corporate staff are specialists and provide counsel and guidance to divisional people. Clearly, the divisions make their own decisions in nearly every phase of the business, and the computer area is no exception.

Although there is a corporate computer staff, under a coordinator of data processing, there are no computers at the corporate headquarters location, or even input-output terminals. There are, however, some 40 computer systems in the company's divisions, and the monthly rental of computers totals $900,000.

Patterns in reporting relationships for the EDP function vary among the divisions. In some, EDP reports to the division controller; in others, it reports to a research scientist, or to an engineer. To some extent the location of responsibility within the divisions depends upon the nature of the division's business, but more important are the status and capability of the person to whom the computer complex reports.

With all of the actual systems work, programming, and computer operations taking place in the divisions, the computer staff at the corporate level has two main tasks: to serve as a loose but effective control on the divisions, discouraging them from applying unnecessary frills or from adopting systems that overlap or conflict with those in other divisions; and to keep up with new computer technology inside and outside of the company and to convince the divisions to adopt certain new methods.

The corporate EDP staff's success depends a great deal on the length of time a particular division has been using a computer. The staff coordinator reports that divisions with only brief computer experience often require considerable "selling" before accepting a new method that the corporate staff believes would be beneficial. On the other hand, divisions with longer experience in EDP are more likely to come to the corporate staff group with new ideas of their own.

The function of the corporate coordinator of data processing is to stimulate interest in new computer applications, to coordinate developments in the data processing field among the divisions, and to hold meetings at which computer people from the divisions meet and exchange views. He also reviews requests for EDP equipment that involve more than $10,000 a year, but the decision of the division manager prevails if there is difference of opinion. About 95 percent of equipment requests involve no argument at all, and with the remaining 5 percent the question generally stems from lack of understanding rather than from deep-seated, conceptual differences.

Because of the diversity among divisions, computer objectives and applications vary greatly from division to division. In some highly technical research and production divisions, EDP usage is largely scientific; in other divisions, business applications predominate. In the larger divisions, however, the split between scientific and business applications is about even, because all corporate functions are requesting comparable amounts of information in one or the other of these broad categories.

Headquarters executives know that the divisions have certain information, and since much of it is, or can be, computerized,

they are now asking for more information than they did ten years ago. For example, the corporate tax people ask for divisional tax information and other reports that require the use of the computer; other functions within the corporate group ask for various ratios for control purposes. Some reports, such as payrolls for the central bank account, are generated directly for the corporate group by computers in the divisions; others, such as corporate forecasts, are based on divisional data that are consolidated by computers.

In this company the responsibility for computer activity is rooted in the divisions. While the corporate staff is expected to coordinate, it operates on the principle that "only the user knows what output he needs and should get." Accordingly, the corporate computer staff is careful not to appear to pressure divisions to accept a particular program.

From the management's standpoint, the mere presence of the corporate staff "looking over a division's shoulder" is believed to lead divisional EDP people to be more precise in their assessments of EDP needs and to resolve many differences in the division before they become issues at the corporate level.

Case 14:
International Electrical and Electronic Equipment Manufacturer

The company is a large, worldwide manufacturer of a variety of electrical and electronic equipment. Its internal organization is somewhat complex. At the core are the operating divisions, each based on a product, a market (defined as an industry or governmental unit, not as a geographical region), or a service.

There are also functional divisions, such as manufacturing, marketing, personnel, and finance; some of these functions exist at the corporate level only, but others extend to the operating divisions. For example, there is a personnel function in each operating division and at corporate headquarters, but the commercial development division is part of the corporate headquarters organization only, and is not present in the operating divisions.

Functional activities within operating divisions are under the direction of the division manager, but each activity also has a strong functional relationship with the corresponding headquarters activity. Thus the corporate data processing head exercises guidance over divisional data processing. Some of the operating divisions and functional divisions have regional groupings that are almost like divisions within divisions.

The divisions enjoy a significant degree of autonomy in that they develop their own profit plans and the like, and there is little transfer of personnel between them.

The company has used electronic data processing equipment for some 20 years; first, largely in production, and then in information and communications. The initial applications in the information and communications area were primarily in accounting; hence, the EDP activity was located, until 1966, in the divisional and corporate controller's offices, under the vice president and treasurer. Today, at both corporate and divisional levels, there is a fairly high level of sophistication in both planning and implementation of computer applications.

The location of the computer complex within the organization and the responsibility for development of the computer-based management information system appear to be in a transitional stage, and the final answers have not yet evolved. Company management has divided activities relating to the EDP-based information system into two parts—information systems and data processing. The vice president and treasurer has retained the responsibility for developing and expanding the business information systems, but a new position, that of vice president of data processing systems, has been created to handle the technical side of data processing—hardware, software, systems programming, and the like.

The respective responsibilities of these two executives were described in a policy statement by the chief executive officer:

> The vice president of data processing systems is responsible for developing and implementing a companywide data processing equipment master plan; for directing the effective utilization of data processing equipment and its application to information processing throughout the company; and for ensuring that the corporate headquarters data processing system utilizes the most modern and efficient techniques. The vice president and treasurer is responsible for developing a unified control and information system encompassing all segments of the company and for developing and maintaining a corporate master plan to coordinate the information systems for measurement, planning, and control.

In most of the divisions the data processing/information systems activity reports to a functional unit, usually finance or accounting, and there is a strong dotted-line relationship to the corporate controller. However, in at least one division, with three vice presidents reporting to the division president, the data processing information systems activity is under one of the vice presidents, who numbers administration among his responsibilities. But the EDP activity is also subject to guidance from the vice president of data processing systems.

As one executive describes the situation, "Data processing is centralized at corporate headquarters but decentralized on a corpo-

rate, companywide basis with the divisions."
A number of the functional and operating
divisions have their own comprehensive
management information systems. In the
operating divisions these tend to be divisionwide systems that serve divisional management in much the same way that the
headquarters system serves corporate management. The largest division also controls
a data base that is used by the other divisions and by corporate headquarters. To a
considerable degree the reorganization of
the data processing/information systems
function at corporate headquarters and the
creation of a corporate information system
were undertaken to accomplish at the corporate level what already had been achieved
in several of the divisions.

Within the company a number of reasons
are advanced for the present location of the
computer complex as an independent unit
and for the division of responsibilities:

1. Data processing was established as a
   separate function to give it exposure.
   Corporate staff people say that the
   function's independent status emphasizes to all managers the importance of
   utilizing the computer in the management process. Further, they maintain,
   this arrangement enables the corporate
   EDP group to foster and maintain ex-
   cellence in computer use. The direction the corporate staff gives to the
   operating and functional groups, it is
   believed, raises the level of computer
   utilization throughout the company.

2. The independent status gives user divisions ready access to the headquarters
   computer complex, as companywide
   needs for, and use of, the information
   system grow.

3. The need for a companywide information system called for a broader approach than any existing functional
   unit could take. A number of EDP personnel in user divisions stated that, as

users, they believed a separate data
processing unit would be more likely
to take a corporate view of developing
EDP applications than would a particular existing function to which the
computer might be assigned. Although
this reason is not subscribed to by financial people, it is one advanced by
several executives in other functional
areas.

4. Clearly, one of the factors in the assignment of responsibilities was the need
   for the data processing function to cut
   across organizational lines. Although
   the controller's function does this,
   management believed that an independent unit could give the necessary direction more effectively through
   its concentration on the technical aspects of EDP. As the company's chief
   executive officer sums up management's thinking, "We can combine the
   advantages of decentralized management with the economies of a unified
   corporate information system."

Under the vice president and treasurer.

Within the finance function, two units
are concerned with the informational aspects of data processing:

- Among his accounting and financial duties, the controller has responsibility
  for the development of policies and
  procedures for accounting, control of
  income and expense, pricing, information systems, and planning, and for
  seeing that these are implemented by
  the operating and functional divisions.

- The director of information systems is
  responsible for directing the development of a unified information and control system, which serves and includes
  all segments of the company; for developing and maintaining a corporate systems plan to accomplish this; for deter-

mining the systems design needed to provide corporate management with the information for planning and control, reporting, and decision making; and for providing staff direction to the corporate headquarters and to the operating and functional divisions to ensure that the data content and design of their systems meet management's requirements.

Under the vice president of data processing systems.

This executive is charged with the following general responsibilities:

- Achieving effective use of data processing equipment and related computer systems and programming functions within the company.
- Developing a corporate plan to coordinate the use of data processing equipment within the company.
- Providing staff direction to executives throughout the company who are engaged in, or affected by, the data processing plan.
- Providing specialized services to corporate headquarters and other groups in the company for centralized applications and for the company's internal communications network.
- Furthering the understanding and use of advanced applications and advanced computer techniques throughout the company.

The data processing systems unit includes the functions that usually go with the operations of a computer facility—computer operations, communications, programming, and the like. But the major thrust of activities emanates from the data processing systems development department; this key department has some 150 employees now, and as the demand for applications grows, the number is increasing.

As part of his drive to improve computer effectiveness in all parts of the company, the vice president of data processing systems has established companywide data processing standards. All orders for electronic data processing equipment are subject to approval by his organization. Similarly, software operations are evaluated for compatibility with the overall data processing standards. This requirement is aimed at the establishment of a consistent standard that will permit adaptation of one division's applications to similar uses in other areas, thereby facilitating the expansion of the companywide management information system.

Development of information systems in most of the divisions continues to be the responsibility of the divisional controller. Potential EDP applications related to the controllers' functions are subject to review by the corporate controller. In addition, the director of information systems at the corporate level assesses proposed applications from the standpoint of the company information system. In those divisions where the data processing/information systems activity was under the controller before the reorganization of the EDP function, the activity was left there, at least for the time being.

The issue of centralization. Through the reorganization of the data processing/information systems function, company management intended to provide more centralized direction and guidance of computer activities throughout the company. Inevitably, the reorganization has encouraged centralization of computer activities in the corporate headquarters, and there is evidence that this trend will continue, although the ultimate extent of centralization is not yet apparent. There is some divisional expectation that a centralized "service" computer facility, with the divisions as users, will evolve, but several corporate executives insist that there is no such plan. Like most managements of divisionalized companies, they believe that a centralized operation would bring adverse reaction from the company's rather autonomous divisions.

Despite corporate management's concern, executives of a number of the major functional and operating divisions applaud the centralizing moves of the past two years, believing that a strong central organization is needed to utilize the computer's potential fully. Subordinate divisional executives express less enthusiasm for centralization.

In one aspect of the company's EDP operations, a fully centralized facility does exist. A telecomputer center, housed at corporate headquarters, operates primarily as a message-switching center for the entire company, serving somewhat as a traffic policeman. Using an IBM 7740/1410, the system controls terminals throughout the United States, Canada, and Europe. One of its functions is to accept data from one location's terminal and to distribute these appropriately to various other terminals; another is to collect data arriving at different times from a number of terminals and prepare them for processing on a user organization's system.

From this center, data for the management information system can be extracted. Further, the center can find a given product or part within the company at any location and notify the inquiring terminal of its nearest location. In the near future the company plans to convert this system to an IBM 360, which will be able to talk not only to the terminal locations but to divisional computers. This capability will be a further step toward centralization and toward the expansion of the companywide management information system.

Development of applications. For a number of years the company has employed computer-based operating systems as management tools in such areas as production control, payroll, and various planning and control systems. Pertinent data from these operating systems add to the companywide management information system. The corporate system permits simulation, trend analysis, and other projective exercises that enable management to systematically use comprehensive information in reaching the broad decisions needed in directing the enterprise.

As the corporate group works on the projected companywide information and control system, a number of divisions continue to piece together segments of their own management information systems, as they have done for several years. The personnel function, for example, has begun work on a man-job matching system and on central compilation of recruiting data. But now, there is greater corporate coordination of systems and applications throughout the company. Some of the functional and operating divisions are able to design, develop, and program their own systems and applications; others are working closely with the headquarters data processing systems division; still others have gone outside the company to consultants for systems analysis and programming work.

Handling of priorities. Time on the computers in the corporate complex is said to be available to users in sufficient quantity, but the time of the corporate and divisional EDP personnel is severely limited. Assignment of corporate data processing systems people for systems and programming work on potential applications sought by user divisions poses some problems. Priority status is subject to continuous review; existing projects are evaluated against new ones, and at times current projects are downgraded in favor of incoming applications. In general, those projects that will yield a quicker return in cost savings, profit potential, or control are given higher priority than those with a longer-term payout. Also considered is the contribution of the proposed application to the corporate management information system. Indeed, when a particular application is needed to further the aim of a companywide information system, the corporate data processing group may urge a division to rearrange its own priority listing. The corporate group recognizes, however, that some applications can be handled more effectively by the functional or operating division than by the central unit, and takes this into account. The data processing unit at headquarters is considering making greater use of systems people in the divisions and beefing up the capabilities already there to relieve some of the time pressures on the central group.

In summary, this is a company that has a history of strong divisional experience and autonomy in data processing, which, as the result of top management decision, is developing a broader management information system. To speed this development, data processing and the information system have been identified as two distinct but highly interrelated functions. The corporate staff provides guidance and evaluation of divisional EDP applications. But because of the capabilities present in the divisions —their history of developing their own systems or purchasing outside support for systems development—and because of the company's continuing divisional philosophy, the corporate data processing and information groups' relationships with the divisions entail as much selling and convincing as directing and controlling.

Case 15:
International Chemical Manufacturer

This international company is organized around highly autonomous product and service divisions that report to the president and the management committee. Operating within the broad context of company policies, each product division is responsible for its own manufacturing, marketing, research and development, engineering, and employee relations. There is, however, a central treasurer's division, which reports to the finance committee. The intent is to give the product divisions great operating and administrative freedom while exercising financial restraints through corporate review and approval of operating budgets.

The decentralization and divisional autonomy that characterize the company are reflected in the evolution of its computer operations.

The company always used tabulating equipment extensively, but in the mid-1950's the engineering division decided to use an early Univac to maintain and expand its engineering services and programs. This decision spurred the treasurer's division to use the computer for processing its voluminous financial and accounting data. The interest of these two groups led to their jointly operating a Univac computer for a two-year experimental period, during which they made a study of their future needs and the feasibility of computerization. At the conclusion of this study, it was apparent that there was sufficient current and potential need for EDP in the accounting and engineering areas to justify additional equipment. Therefore, engineering took over the Univac, and the accounting department in the treasurer's division acquired an IBM 705.

During the two-year study period, and partially as a result of the experimentation with the Univac, other divisions and plants studied the potential value and application of computers to their operations. As a result the use of data processing and the acquisition of computers expanded throughout the company. Most divisions and plants, asserting their autonomy, set up their own com-

EXHIBIT P. *Organization of Computer Activity — Corporate Business Systems Department*

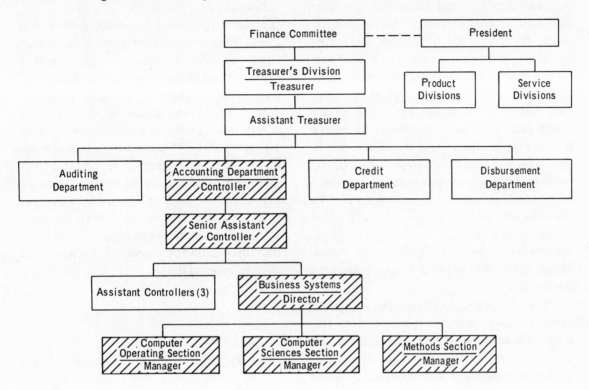

puter operations, but a number elected to use the computer complex in the accounting department for business data applications; some divisions used the engineering division's computer for both business and technical applications.

The accounting department's computer complex currently processes 50 percent of the company's EDP work and is striving for greater centralization of computer operations without challenging divisional autonomy. Responsibility resides in the business systems department, under the director of business systems, a position comparable in level to an assistant controller. These relationships and the organizational location of the business systems department are illustrated in Exhibit P.

In keeping with the centralization of the treasurer's function, the business systems function in the corporate accounting department is duplicated in each divisional

controller's department as a business analysis section. But these sections are free to pursue autonomous computer operations. They are responsible to the corporate accounting department to the extent that they must provide required data in a prescribed format at specified times.

The number of personnel in product-divisional computer operations ranges from 1 to 2 programmers in one division to 10 to 15 systems people in another. Some of the larger and more complex plants may have even larger complements of computer personnel; for example, one plant has 20 systems people in the business data area and 10 in technical data processing.

The corporate business systems department acts as an internal service bureau and encourages other divisions to make greater use of its computer center. It offers a broad range of services, from actual processing of data to assignment of personnel for research and development of both computer and noncomputer business systems, a function that some divisions cannot do themselves. In short, the corporate department attempts to demonstrate to the divisions that it can take over their existing data processing work and meet their requirements at a lower cost, and at the same time can facilitate the development of new programs or adapt existing programs to the division's needs. Accordingly, the corporate department makes frequent presentations to the directors of divisional control functions and to division general managers—especially when a new general manager or division controller has been appointed, or when plans are being made for acquiring new computer hardware.

Over the years, 18 divisional computer installations have been transferred to the corporate business systems department. In turn, this group has agreed to absorb the divisions' computers and tabulating equipment and their data processing personnel. Excess personnel have been either assimilated in expanded operations or balanced out by attrition. The user divisions are charged for data processing services and for the development of programs or applications. There is no charge for investigating and exploring potential programs and applications; these are supported by a sizable budget for research and development.

Divisional users may insist upon a particular system or application even though its effectiveness is questioned by corporate business systems personnel. The division's autonomy and willingness to pay the cost are the determining factors in the final decision.

As part of its overall responsibility the corporate business systems department develops advanced programming techniques, conducts courses in computer technology and programming, and publishes standards manuals. It offers these services to all divisions, but it must rely on their proving

valuable to users in order to promote their adoption by the divisions.

Despite the trend toward centralization there is little corporate control over purchase or lease of major computer equipment, although each division or plant first secures management approval, as it does for other capital expenditures. An advisory committee, composed of the ten largest divisional users of business data and the ten largest potential users of technical equipment, serves as a clearinghouse to disseminate information on the capability and potential of new hardware. There is also a software advisory committee, which is active in evaluating needs of divisions for various types of data.

Case 16:
Airline

Even though the company is the result of mergers and acquisitions, operationally it is totally centralized, in the sense that there are no regional or product divisions. In management's view, the company's business—the movement of passengers and freight—is not compatible with the concept of divisionalization. Thus a centralized organization was a reality in this company long before any approach to a centralized electronic data processing operation was conceived.

The company has been familiar with electronic data processing for a long time. As early as 1931, punched-card devices were used in the accounting department. Later, sorters and collators were introduced, and the company quickly advanced to computers and wired program boards. Among the early computer applications were ticket accounting, payroll, general accounting, personnel record keeping, and inventory control. In 1957 the company adopted the concept of stored programs when it put payroll accounting on an IBM 650.

Although EDP was first used in accounting, applications moved beyond the accounting function at an early date. Inventory and availability of seats were placed on IBM's RAMAC 305 in 1958, and a Bendix G-15 computer was introduced two years later to calculate flight plans. These were all off-line operations.

The real-time concept was first applied in 1960, when the seats inventory and availability data were stored on magnetic tape. Since then, the company has kept pace with developments in computer technology, and it now has a Univac system, including automatic message switching, that enables it to handle reservations control and flight planning on an on-line, real-time basis.

As the capabilities and flexibility of computers improved, company management began to consider additional EDP applications. In 1965 top management identified 17 functions that might benefit from computer applications, and an economic evaluation was made on how the computer would benefit each one. To tap this potential, a separate department of information services, which incorporated a number of systems formerly under the controllers' authority, was set up under a vice president. The new department was given a broad charter for developing computer-based management information systems covering most of the vital functions of the business, but processing of purely financial data remained under the controller.

Today, the EDP activity is largely, although not totally, centralized. There are two major data processing installations and one minor one.

The minor EDP-based system is in flight operations. It has elements of an information system but is really an operating system, and in a manufacturing business it would be tied to production. The system generates information for flight planning, flight monitoring, and calculating gross flight weights.

Financial accounting, under the controller, is a separate system with its own computer installations at two local but widely separated spots. In addition to being responsible for the standard elements of modern financial accounting, the controller supervises the inventory-control system, a highly significant system for an airline because of the importance of the availability and the high cost of replacement parts. The organization of the data processing function under the controller and its component units are shown in Exhibits Q, R, S, and T.

The other major data processing operation is in the information services department, which has jurisdiction over all data processing except the accounting and the flight operations systems. It is this information services system that this study is primarily concerned with, and it is described in detail below.

Over and above the factors favoring centralization of the company operationally, two conditions would have led to centralization of the data processing capability, regardless of the company's overall management mode. First, since the primary consideration of the airline is its passengers, one of the paramount tasks of the information system is to support the reservations function throughout the network of company operations. This process, which must be real-time, can be accomplished best on a centralized basis that permits the information flowing out of the passenger reservation activity to be used in other areas. Second, as is true of all airlines, the company has access to privately owned communications facilities providing a broad array of communication devices. These facilities, owned in common by the airlines, utilize large chunks of telephone lines obtained from the telephone company at a reduced rate. Their cost is then prorated

EXHIBIT Q. *Organization of the Accounting Data Processing Function**

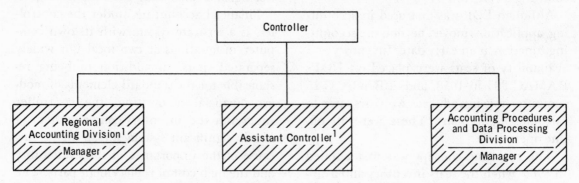

*See Exhibits R, S, and T for organization of component units in the accounting data processing function.
[1] Widely separated geographically from headquarters location.

EXHIBIT R. *Organization of Assistant Controller's Unit — Accounting Data Processing Function*

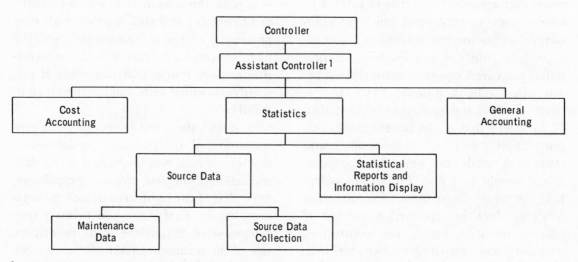

[1] Widely removed geographically from headquarters location.

among the user companies, making the communications cost per company much lower than if the same service were obtained by a company independently. Thus the cost of telecommunications and other means of connecting far-flung terminals to a central computer installation, a significant consideration in most companies, tends to be considerably lower for Case 16 than for nonairline companies or for companies that obtain the lines individually.

For these reasons, and because of the nature of the company's business, the data

processing/information systems organization, already highly centralized, is moving toward even greater centralization. It is expected that eventually the whole EDP-based accounting system and the systems work now being done in user organizations will come under the information services department.

Although company management recognizes the need to have an extremely competent individual at the head of the information systems activity, it regards the location of the function as the primary factor in its effective use. Company executives

EXHIBIT S. *Organization of Regional Accounting Division —*
Accounting Data Processing Functions

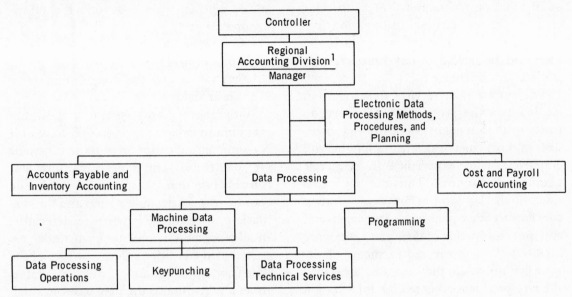

[1] Widely removed geographically from headquarters location.

EXHIBIT T. *Organization of Accounting Procedures and Data Processing Division —*
Accounting Data Processing Function

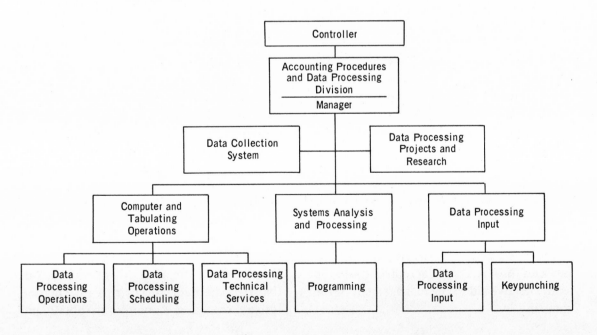

doubt whether the progress that has been achieved could have resulted if the activity had been placed in operations, accounting, or in some other functional area. In their view a general-purpose information system, such as theirs, must cross functional lines and be devoid of any functional organizational orientation.

The information services department is headed by a vice president, who reports directly to the president. Both the vice president and his chief associate are long-service employees with experience in economic planning and control. Thus they have considerable background in conveying abstract concepts to other members of management, and the combination of their past experience blends well with the requirements of the information system they now operate. Until the vice president accepted the information system assignment some three years ago, his only contact with the computer had been as a user.

The vice president's direct reporting relationship to the president was determined by the president at the time the information services department was established. The decision was based on two major considerations:

- The system should cut across departmental and functional lines; therefore, the executive who heads it should have the necessary stature and should not be restricted to focusing on any particular function or functional department.
- The key to evaluating and modifying the system and potential data processing applications is to assess their payback to the total company—a matter that can be determined only at the top.

Thus the system and its applications not only have the stamp of top management, as indicated by the reporting relationship, but they also have been accepted at the top as an effective aid to the management of the company.

The organization of the information services department and of its major component units is shown in Exhibits U, V, W, and X. The department includes the following operations:

- Computer operations.
- Communications.
- Systems analysis and programming.
- Technical services.

With respect to the systems analysis and programming department, shown in Exhibit X, some amplification of certain functions may be helpful. The projects planning and control function is concerned with the coordination of documentation and the simulation of a proposed system to determine in advance how it will perform under expected load conditions. The manager of the data-base programming division establishes and maintains the data base on which the system rests. The applications planning division establishes conventions and specifications for the design and development of user applications; it also evaluates user requests for new applications on the basis of cost benefit to be realized, underlying philosophy, and the like. An assistant to the director handles the business aspects of the department's operations, such as budgets and requisitions, and works closely with the vice president's administrative assistant.

Although the EDP operation supporting the information system is now highly centralized, user organizations play significant roles in the determination and design of computer applications for their own areas. Some do their own systems work. More important, however, is the realization by all concerned that no system is good unless it meets standards of both the user and the information services department. The information services staff believe that it is the user's responsibility to identify the information needed to manage his operation, but that it is their job to put this information into a form that is economical to obtain and

EXHIBIT U. *Organization of the Information Services Department**

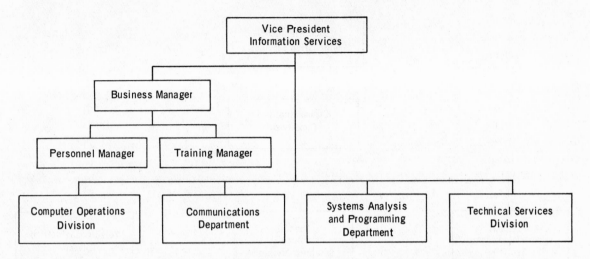

*See Exhibits V, W, and X for organization of component units in the information services department.

EXHIBIT V. *Organization of the Computer Operations Division — Information Services Department*

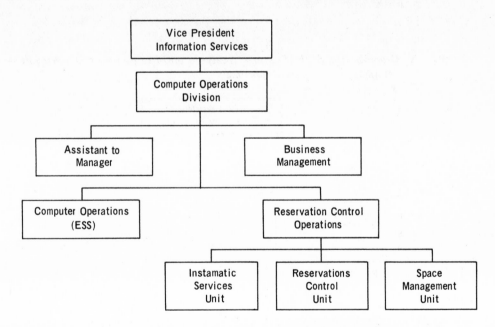

use, is within the proper time frame of reference, and is applicable to the user's needs.

In the department's formative stages the vice president invited 29 representatives of potential user organizations to participate in a task force that was assisting in launching the department. Through this device the vice president gained insight into how prospective "customers" would use the computer. At the end of a seven-month period, during which the task force met full time, expending more than 200 man-months, it had compiled a complete library of specifications for meeting the needs of computer users. From these specifications of functional needs, the computer group compiled pro-

EXHIBIT W. *Organization of the Communications Department – Information Services Department*

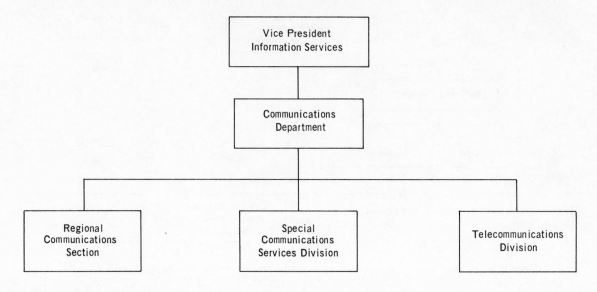

EXHIBIT X. *Organization of the Systems Analysis and Programming Department –*
Information Services Department

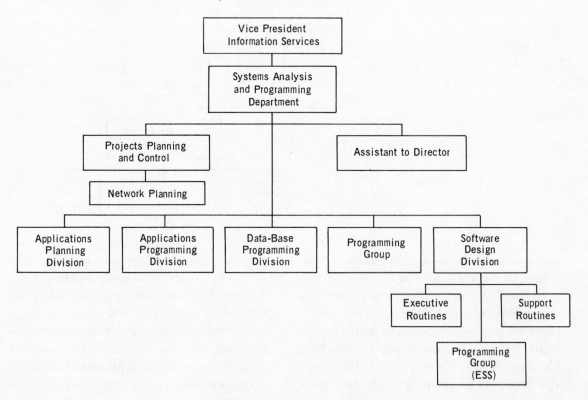

gramming specifications. But they still needed procedure and training specifications for those who would be using the functional and programming handbooks. A new committee was formed, with many of the original task-force participants as members. In this way the users were deeply involved in the process of the information services department, at least in its formative period, despite its highly centralized nature.

The basic objectives of the information services department are:

- To provide information for operations, marketing, and services.
- To supply all managers with the information they need in planning the selling of service.
- To give general management the information that it needs for long-range corporate planning.

Overall, the vice president of information services sees his job as one of aiding the various departments to find new and better ways of improving service to the customer. Sometimes it is his role to identify these better ways and to offer a user a number of alternative methods of improvement and then sell him on the most effective one. In the present system there is enough room for growth to ensure that company needs can be met for several years; the system's specifications were designed for maximum flexibility and with the capacity for handling double the company's estimated 1970 volume.

Data processing in the information system includes the following:

- A real-time passenger reservations service.
- A message-switching system.
- A performance-analysis system.
- A passenger name-record system.

In addition the system will soon include eight new applications. Some 17 proposed applications are also in the offing. Nothing essential to the old computer-based system

has been eliminated; rather, this system has been incorporated into the new information system. Although the reports derived for management from the real-time, on-line applications are now fallout from the main activity, they, and the data used in compiling them, would have to be gathered anyway, even in the absence of the real-time applications.

At no time has the information services staff lost sight of the relationship between the technical side of its function and the basic objectives of the department. It has viewed the continued advances in hardware design only as a means of improving the job of information handling.

With the vast amount of data available to management, and with the increasing speed of information handling, members of top management and the vice president of information services and his staff are aware of the dangers of "experting" from headquarters. They all work hard to prevent this. The basic philosophy of management in the company is opposed to detailed direction from headquarters. The belief in the company is that as the information available through the system sharpens middle management's ability to make decisions, the decision-making leeway will be enhanced. Also, exceptions will become known to the middle manager earlier, and various alternatives for dealing with them will be available to him.

Acquisition of hardware. When the information services department was organized, a vendor-evaluation team was formed to recommend the selection of a computer system. This team consisted of a project leader from the operations research group, a representative of the communications department who was informed on hardware, an expert in passenger reservations, a representative from customer service, and a software expert from the company's extant computer-based reservation system. This team reported to a steering committee chaired by the vice president of management services and composed of the vice president of communications, the vice president of purchasing, the director of the reservations department, and the controller. On the recommendation of both groups, a Univac system was selected for the electronic information system and a CDC system for long-range flight planning. Now that the information services department is operational, the acquisition of hardware related to the information system is the responsibility of the vice president of that department and his staff.

Systems development. Systems design and development is not quite as highly centralized as the operation of the computer facility and the programming function. Systems are designed in a few of the user departments by systems-oriented people working with staff members of the information services department. This small degree of decentralization is, in part, an attempt to relate the users' needs more closely to the systems developed. The philosophy of the information services department is that it is up to the user to determine what information he needs to facilitate the management of his department.

Any system designed by a user must meet configuration specifications administered by the EDP staff. Information services weighs requests from user departments for computer applications on the basis of their potential contribution to the profitability of the company and their value to users. An application that may not show much promise on a purely economic basis may offer a better way of providing service to customers, and may be developed for this reason.

The vice president of information services plays a dominant role in establishing priorities among competing proposed computer applications. However, a difference over priorities is resolved by the vice president and the head of the user department in question. When these two cannot resolve the issue, the president makes the decision.

The information services department is now moving from a position in which it had to develop uses for the computer to one in which it must select from among several proposed applications. Currently, it has requests for a number of applications from such functions as engineering, market research, and personnel. At this point the EDP staff is concerned that if it cannot get to these applications within the next year or so, the initial momentum may disappear and dissatisfaction will result from the lack of immediate action.

Recruitment and training of EDP personnel. The information services department differs from the EDP organizations of other companies in that it has formalized the personnel and training aspects of its operation. It has recruited not only from within the company but also from outside. The department found that it could tolerate about 40 percent of its staff to be inexperienced as programmers if the remaining 60 percent were experienced. The 40 percent generally are employees with company experience, and the 60 percent have usually been hired from outside.

Ninety employees with an interest in, and aptitude for, EDP work were selected to attend a three-week course in EDP, including general concepts and FORTRAN programming, which was conducted by the department's training staff. Twenty-one of these were picked to become programmers, and many of them are now sophisticated systems-programmers; the other 69 returned to their own departments where, at the time of this study, all but six had received promotions. Thus the company has a backlog of employees with some training in EDP programming who have carried an understanding of EDP applications back to their own departments.

Managers in the information services organization believe that systems analysts and programmers tend to be a breed apart, and that this is one of the reasons they work well in their occupation. In order not to stifle these people's special abilities, department managers are striving to foster a work atmosphere that is conducive to creativity but that also ensures that standards are maintained. To accomplish this balance, there is considerable individual counseling and frank discussion between each man and his boss. But the managers readily acknowledge that there is no short-cut to meshing the two goals.

The vice president of information services is convinced that service in his department is excellent training for higher-management positions. He points out that the traits of intelligence and creativity, which are needed for EDP work, are also sought throughout the organization. Moreover, the young systems analyst or programmer, through his exposure to the company as a whole, is able to reach beyond the confines of his immediate job and to broaden his knowledge. To date, however, EDP training has not been translated into any formal approach to management development.

Like other EDP managers, the vice president of information services has an educational job to do among his fellow managers. But he believes his task is somewhat easier than most, since management in this company has a long tradition of adopting the newest and most effective management tools. For example, the company undertook a work plan in 1940, profit planning in 1941, central regulation editing and central forms control in the 1940's, job evaluation in 1946, a model for use in scheduling line maintenance in 1952, operations research in the mid-1950's, and models for many things since then. A central organization, economic planning, which the vice president of information services once headed, carried on educational activities among management personnel to develop the use of the new management tools.

With this strong tradition already established, the atmosphere in which EDP education takes place is considerably more receptive than in many other companies. An educational job must be done, nevertheless, with respect to the specifics of EDP and its applications for user organizations.

This, then, is a company highly centralized in operation through its adaptation to its business environment, and it has a strong innovative streak. Though various forms of electronic data processing have long been in use in the company, until 1965 most applications were in the field of accounting. At that time, top management decided that the needed expansion of EDP could not be accomplished within the framework of the accounting function, and it created a separate department to enlarge the information net. A number of the systems formerly under the controller's authority have been incorporated into the information system; however, data processing for purely financial accounting purposes remains apart from the information system's processing and is still under the controller.

The information services department, serving a centralized company, is itself highly centralized, reporting directly to the president and chief executive officer. As with other data processing/information systems organizations, this department is moving toward even greater centralization and consolidation of all data processing activities in the company.

Appendix II. Sample Project Request and
Authorization Forms and
Sample Policy Statement

TABLE A. *Information Systems Project Request*

TO COMPUTER LIAISON MANAGER				
☐ AGRICULTURE	☐ CONSUMER	☐ CORPORATE	☐ INDUSTRIAL	☐ MATERIALS

Project Name	Requested By	Date

Description, Scope, Objectives

EXPECTED BENEFITS

Profit Improvement:

Cost Reduction:

Service:

Total Annual Profit Potential $ _____

ESTIMATED COSTS	APPROVALS
Design and Installation (One Time)	Requestor
Systems Work $ _____	
Machines and Equipment _____	Computer Liaison Manager
Other _____	
TOTAL $ ============	Division Controller
OPERATING (MONTHLY)	Division Manager (Budget Responsibility)
Additional Personnel $ _____	
Machines and Equipment _____	Director, Information Systems & Services
Forms _____	
Other _____	Distribution After Approval
TOTAL $ ============	1. Computer Liaison
	2. Requestor
	3. Division Controller
	4. Division Manager

Project No.	Priority	Project Leader	Scheduled Completion	5. Computer Planning
				6. Computer Research

TABLE B. *Data Processing Systems*
Project Authorization

Systems Analyst		Job No.
Client		Data

Function	Division/Department	Project Title

Project Description

Quantifiable Benefits ☐ Annual ☐ One Time	Estimated	Actual Per Audit
Profit Improvement (reduced exp. or cost, or increased revenue)	$	$
Cost Avoidance	$	$
Increased Resource Utilization or Reduced Cycle Time	$	$
Other Quantifiable Benefit: _____		
Return on Investment	%	%

Nonquantifiable Benefits

Authorized Project Cost	Prel. Estimate of Operating Cost	Account to Charge

Target Code	Project Targets	Due Date	Target Code	Project Targets	Due Date

AUTHORIZATION APPROVALS AND DATE

Applications Manager	Division	Director, Data Processing

CLOSE-OUT APPROVAL AND DATE

Applications Manager	NO CHARGES ACCEPTED AFTER THIS DATE. ←

Audit of Benefits	Audited By
	Date

Typical Company Policy Statement Describing the EDP Function Within a Controller's Department

1. It is essential to coordinate the plans for an application of data processing technology on an over-all company basis in order to obtain the most profitable application of this technology for the company.
2. The corporate controller is responsible for providing the necessary coordination of, and direction to, these plans.
3. The policy shall apply to:
   - Systems or applications development activities which require six man-months or more.
   - Data processing and related equipment, new or replacement, involving a monthly rental of $_____ or more, or purchases with a capital asset value of $_____ or more.
4. The corporate controller will coordinate the designated activities by:
   - Developing, with subsidiary companies and corporate departments, overall long-range objectives for the company's data processing and operations research activities, and by reviewing these plans periodically.
   - Advising subsidiary companies and corporate departments in the preparation of proposed computer applications, and reviewing them for endorsement on the basis of (1) objectives of the project, (2) estimated staff requirements and cost, (3) an evaluation of the benefits, and (4) a schedule of progress dates.
   - Taking the initiative in developing programs and applications of a corporatewide nature, cutting across subsidiary company lines.
   - Establishing companywide standards for methods, programs, languages, and hardware to ensure the required level of compatibility.
   - Reviewing data processing activities with subsidiary companies and corporate departments on a regular basis.
   - Reviewing for endorsement:
     a. Hardware acquisition proposals, in keeping with paragraph 3.
     b. Requests for use of outside consultants and of computer or programming services.
5. The corporate controller will supplement, as needed, the staffs of subsidiary companies and corporate departments for work on major data processing projects by temporary assignment of the corporate EDP staff from the controller's office, and will recommend staffing levels and training methods for subsidiary company and corporate department data processing projects.
6. Subsidiary companies should obtain agreement from the corporate controller with respect to items covered by this policy.

$15.00

BUSINESS

Organizing for Data Processing

Robert R. Reichenbach   •   Charles A. Tasso

Will a computer-based management information system function differently if the responsibility for it rests with the controller rather than with a vice president/operations or a vice president/information systems?

Based on the findings of this study, the answer is that it will. Specifically, the report examines why responsibility in a given company is placed where it is; what effect this assignment has on what the computer does and how well it does it; and what developments are causing changes in the location of computer responsibility as management's need for information continues to expand in both breadth and depth. This pioneering study is based on multiple in-depth interviews with 91 executives representing 16 companies in a wide variety of industries. An extensive appendix provides case histories of computer operations in each company along with samples of policy statements and project request and authorization forms.

Organizing for Data Processing assesses the importance of computer-responsibility locations by examining the relationship of EDP and management information systems, the effect of location on the relevancy of data, the consequences of centralization or divisionalization on the computer complex, the actual operations of the computer complex, and the means of orienting the total organization to the computer complex.

This report is designed to aid management in determining the organizational position of the computer responsibility within their firms so that EDP applications to business systems will serve the aims of their companies in the most effective manner.

American Management Association, Inc.

135 West 50th Street   New York, N.Y. 10020

Cover design by Stuart Silver

03092